Pioneering Spirit

I would like to dedicate this book
to my parents
who were among those whose pioneering spirit
made this province a good place in which to live.

Pioneering Spirit

Ontario Places of Worship, Then and Now

A Personal Journey

Elizabeth Luther

Published in association with
Eglinton St. George's United Church
Toronto, Ontario

eastendbooks
Toronto 2000

The support of the Government of Ontario, through Ontario 2000 and the Ministry of Citizenship, Culture and Recreation, is gratefully acknowledged.

Designed by Shannon MacMillan.
Printed in Canada by Métrolitho.

Front Cover: Chapel of the Mohawks, Brantford.
Back Cover: Islamic Foundation of Toronto, Scarborough; Sand Lake Pioneer Church, Parry Sound; Actinolite United Church, Municipality of Tweed.
All photographs are by the author, unless otherwise acknowledged.

Canadian Cataloguing in Publication Data

Luther, Elizabeth, 1924-
        Pioneering spirit : Ontario places of worship, then and now

Co-published by Eglinton St. George's United Church.
Includes bibliographical references and index.
ISBN 1-896973-20-5

1. Ontario — Church history. 2. Church buildings — Ontario — History.
3. Religious facilities — Ontario — History. I. Eglinton St. George's United Church (Toronto, Ont.). II. Title.

BR575.O5L87 2000   277.13   C00-931837-2

eastendbooks is an imprint of Venture Press
45 Fernwood Park Avenue, Toronto, Ontario, Canada M4E 3E9
Tel: (416) 691-6816; Fax: (416) 691-2414
E-mail: info@eastendbooks.com
VISIT OUR WEBSITE AT www.eastendbooks.com

Contents

Introduction

There is a destiny that makes us brothers;
None goes his way alone,
All that we send into the lives of others
Comes back into our own.

Edwin Markham (1852–1940)

One cloudy day, while hiking through the woods near Lake Eloida in eastern Ontario, I came across an old, abandoned Methodist church. Brush and weeds made up the building's congregation. One purple lilac, a favourite shrub in many nineteenth-century pioneer gardens, gave the lonely structure a jaunty aspect.

I was appalled at the desecration that had taken place. Bottles littered the rubble-strewn floor. The windows were gone; their glass, lying amongst the debris, caught glints of the late afternoon light in some drops of rain. The door, as solid as the old pioneers, swayed drunkenly on its rusted, broken hinges.

As I stood gazing up through the partly demolished roof to the cloudy sky, I wondered about the people who had built that modest house of worship. From what part of the world had they come? What were their dreams when they laid that first cornerstone?

I had ventured into the area hoping to find the log cabin where a local legend known as The Witch of Plum Hollow had lived. Had she been part of the congregation that once filled the now-abandoned church? Her story is remembered, but not the story of the people who built the church. I came away with a sense of sadness that so much of our history is being lost.

After that episode, I became interested in the stories of other such places of worship that are still standing today and that are, for the most part, still active. I began to explore these buildings and their congregations, and to record some of the challenges that confronted the various old and new pioneers who have come to the Canadian

1

province of Ontario.

My interest eventually led to an informal lecture or talk, illustrated with slides, that I presented to church groups across the province. Giving these talks brought home to me how little we often know about our own heritage. There are brave individuals in our past to whom we owe a debt of gratitude. But some of us still don't remember that Sir John A. Macdonald was Canada's first federal prime minister — and very few know where he is buried. Now that my explorations of Ontario pioneer places of worship are being published, it is my hope that the resulting book can play some part in encouraging both current and rising generations to learn more about all the people who have helped build our distinctive Canadian community in Ontario today.

For me, my explorations have been a challenging and fascinating experience. I have met so many interesting and helpful people during my travels across the province. It has been my pleasure to attend services in many of the different houses of worship I have visited. Just by listening, I have learned there is always a story to be told. Though I have always been concerned to get the essential facts straight, I have not hesitated to pass along many of the anecdotes with which I have been regaled. Legendary or real, they too are a part of Ontario's heritage.

The abandoned Methodist church near Lake Eloida.

My interest in the subject began with churches built by the old family farm pioneers of the late eighteenth and earlier nineteenth centuries. Then I started to think about how, in fact, the first pioneers came long before then. By the time my explorations ended, I was also visiting places of worship established by the diverse groups of immigrants from all over the world who continue to settle in Ontario.

This book is about the Ontario that has been and continues to be built by all the pioneers, past and present. Yet my own beginnings have left a mark on the pages that follow. Our rich heritage continues to be enhanced by the multitudes of new pioneers arriving with their dreams. While their stories are of prime importance, as are those of the earliest First Nations and European empires, so are the stories of the early pioneers who laid a strong groundwork for the current landscape of our province, some two hundred years ago.

All told, the book presents more than fifty places of worship from Glengarry County in eastern Ontario to old Kent County in the southwest, and from present-day multicultural Toronto all the way to Moosonee in the far north. The choice of the places of worship included has been influenced, of course, by my own interests. Many beautiful, historic, or interesting churches have not been included simply because I did not come across them in my travels. I have visited many more houses of worship than the ones profiled here, and I wish I could have included them all. The final choice came down to the ones I considered to have the most interesting stories attached to them, since my book is more about the people who make up the congregations than about the buildings themselves. The general order of presentation is chronological, by age of building. I have allowed myself to stray from the straightest and narrowest understanding of this path, however, when other more particular factors seemed to call for it.

I have also tried to include enough geographical information in the headings to make it possible for those who may wish to visit the buildings themselves to do so. Maps showing the locations of the places of worship appear at the end of the text.

Meanwhile, it has been suggested to me that this is as much a journey through Ontario history, via its religious institutions, as it is an account of places of worship in their own right, and I think this is true. Readers of this book are about to embark on a trip through time.

Acknowledgements

I am pleased to acknowledge that *Pioneering Spirit* has been published under the sponsorship of Eglinton St. George's United Church in Toronto (of which I am a member myself) as a millennium project generously supported by the Ministry of Citizenship, Culture and Recreation through the Ontario 2000 program. I am grateful to the United Church Women of Eglinton St. George's for sponsoring this book. Special thanks to Joyce Johnson, past president of the organization, for her unfailing support.

There are so many people all across the province who have willingly given me their time and encouragement. Whenever I contacted staff at the various religious organizations, I was extended every courtesy. I have attended many of their services and shared in their social hours.

Among the many houses of worship that welcomed me was the Sikh Society. Puneet Kahli, a delightful young man, picked me up and gave me a tour of their temple in Mississauga. The administrator of the Islamic Foundation of Toronto, Farooq Khan, showed me through their mosque. I met with Mr. Moorthy, president of the Hindu Temple Society of Canada, in their temple. He reviewed my material and gave me the sketch of the building's planned exterior. David Hart, archivist of Holy Blossom Temple, spent time with me and provided me with documents from their library. I am indebted to Reverend Pho Timh of Hoa Nghiem Temple for allowing me to use her story. Father Paul and staff provided background material for the Greek Orthodox Church of St. George. I met with Fred Sneyd, son of Robert Sneyd, who explained the symbols in the memorial window of Calvary Baptist Church. Chris Burke, administrator, welcomed me to Christ the King Cathedral in Moosonee. All of these people contributed material that enabled me to include their house of worship in my work, and for that I thank them.

I did not personally visit three of the churches included in this book. My thanks to my friends Bill Cody and his daughter Leslie for providing me with information about and pictures of St. Matthew's Anglican Church in Ottawa. I am grateful to the staff of St. Peter's Roman Catholic Church in Thunder Bay, who sent me material and photographs. Although I had visited the two churches in Williamstown, I did not hear about the nearby ruins of St. Raphaels Roman Catholic Church until much later. My thanks to Colleen Kennedy, president of the Friends of the Ruins of St. Raphaels, for giving me permission to use the photograph from their website. Thanks also to Rand Paterson, who found photographs of l'Église Sacré-Coeur de Jésus in Corbeil before it was destroyed by fire.

I am indebted to Professor Sheila McDonough of Concordia University for her advice on the Islamic faith. Jean Peacock very graciously loaned me family records pertaining to the Congregational Church in St. Elmo. Throughout my research, the staff of the George Locke Public Library, particularly Lorna Scott, were unceasing in their efforts to help. Whenever I needed source material, they were always ready to aid me in my search.

I have tried my family's patience on many occasions by returning to the same church more than once to re-take photographs and to gather more information. I recognize that standing around twiddling one's thumbs while someone else is really enjoying what she is doing can be tedious. It was always a pleasure to have my sister, Kathleen Empey, accompany me on my expeditions. Her support never lagged. Thank you for simply being there.

Thanks to Shannon MacMillan, who was in charge of editing my material and who kept me pointed in the right direction. Thanks also to Randall White of eastendbooks, who used his historical expertise to ensure that I got the details right.

My sincere thanks and appreciation to Jeanne MacDonald at eastendbooks. When I said, "I can't do that because I don't know anything about it," she replied, "Just do it." Her gentle encouragement has been invaluable, and I've truly enjoyed the time we've spent working together.

In the Beginning

The First Nations were of course the first spiritual pioneers. Yet the written or recorded story of what we now call Ontario begins more exactly when the aboriginal peoples of the present-day province first encountered new arrivals from across the sea, in the early seventeenth century. If we could somehow travel back to that point in time, we would not notice any skyscrapers or cities or even rugged roads through growing districts of large family farms. We would see a land where the lynx, wolf, deer, bear, and moose roamed freely, and fish, otter, muskrat, and beaver glided through a vast network of lakes and rivers. A country of enormous forests, populated by a diverse assortment of aboriginal communities, whose inhabitants travelled and traded by canoe, would greet our eyes. We would marvel at the Great Lakes and Niagara Falls. Ontario's first people would point out the beauty of the water roaring over the brink, and we would stand in awe at the pristine natural splendour.

Though groups from other parts of the world would appear soon enough, most of the early new arrivals in this natural paradise were from Europe (and especially from France, England, and Holland). The old French empire led the first European contacts with the Huron Confederacy and its neighbours in present-day central Ontario. Catholic Christian missionaries played a prominent part at first. The First Nations had their own spiritual beliefs and practices, and their own sacred places — a few of which still mark the Ontario landscape. Some seventeenth-century Huron, however, did convert to Christianity. The Jesuit Fathers have left a rich record of the adventure, and buildings have subsequently been constructed (and reconstructed) to commemorate this early written history.

From the saga of the Huron Confederacy and the Jesuit Fathers down to the late eighteenth century, modern Ontario was in its birth throes. The main stories are the growth of the pioneering "Indian and European" fur trade in Canada, and the long struggle between France and England (and their various First Nations allies) over the destiny of the North American Great Lakes. By the 1780s an influx of refugees from the former British American colonies, bringing their various forms of Christianity, had announced the arrival of new pioneers and the beginning of a new era "north of the lakes." Among these refugees was Joseph Brant, leading the loyal Six Nations Iroquois of what is now upstate New York to land along the Grand River in Ontario. One of the Six Nations with a long history as valued allies of the British Crown — the Mohawks — erected a Protestant Christian place of worship that is still standing today.

Simcoe County

1. Sainte-Marie-au-pays-des-Hurons, 1639
Highway 12, Midland

> 'Twas in the moon of winter time,
> When all the birds had fled,
> That mighty Gitchi Manitou
> Sent angel choirs instead.
>
> Father Jean de Brébeuf (1593–1649)

Although Our Lady of the Assumption Church in Windsor claims to be the oldest Roman Catholic church in Ontario, it was not the first. That honour is probably best awarded to Sainte-Marie-au-pays-des-Hurons, near present-day Midland.

In 1615, shortly after Samuel de Champlain's arrival at the fortified Huron town of Carhagouha (just west of Midland), the Récollet priest, Father Le Caron, built a temporary altar and held the first Catholic Mass in Ontario. But the Jesuit fathers who would finally build Sainte-Marie would not arrive in the Huron country between Lake Simcoe and Georgian Bay for another ten years. It was not until the summer of 1639 that the Jesuits obtained permission from their Huron hosts to build a mission and central residence on the banks of the Wye River.

A place for rest and retreat, Sainte-Marie was set apart from the habitations of the Huron. The Blackrobes, as the Huron called the Jesuits, saw Sainte-Marie as a centre for all Huronia, and they built a hospital, a cemetery, a place apart where non-believers could hear "the word," and a chapel. For almost a decade the mission settlement on the banks of the Wye River prospered. Gardens were planted and livestock transported by canoe from Québec. By 1647 there were eighteen French Catholic priests and twenty-four laymen in the Huron country. St. Joseph's Chapel, the "House of Peace" at Sainte-Marie, became a centre of spiritual guidance for those Huron who converted to Christianity.

Alas, during these years the Huron also faced grim epidemics that dramatically reduced their population, and a relentless struggle with their mortal enemies, the Iroquois, for control of the rising fur trade. In 1648 and 1649 the Huron suffered a series of crushing defeats. In March 1649 the Jesuit priests, Fathers Jean de Brébeuf and

Sainte-Marie-au-pays-des Hurons, Midland.

Gabriel Lalemant, were captured, tortured, and put to death, along with hundreds of Huron converts. In May Sainte-Marie itself was burned by its inhabitants, to prevent its falling into enemy hands. The Jesuits and some Huron retreated to St. Joseph's Island (Christian Island today) in Georgian Bay. Here the Jesuits established a second Sainte-Marie, but it would last only a year. The Jesuits and some faithful Huron finally fled to the safety of Québec. Other Huron fled to the north and west. (Others again were absorbed into the ranks of the Iroquois.) Father Paul Ragueneau would write, "It was not without tears that we left a country which we loved, a country watered with the blood of our brothers."

Some three hundred years later, after the Second World War, archaeological excavations began to uncover the physical remains of this early history. In the 1960s the government of Ontario took an interest in restoring and reconstructing Sainte-Marie as a historical site. Today, Sainte-Marie-au-pays-des-Hurons is a wonderfully restored living legend of seventeenth-century Ontario. The reconstruction is painstakingly accurate. The workmen sometimes used the same kinds of tools as the original builders. Rough logs form the walls. Two wooden crosses grace the gable ends of the steeply pitched cedar-shake roof. Inside the reconstructed St. Joseph's Chapel are two altars — one where the priests would make their daily devotions, the other for members of the congregation.

The bones of Fathers Jean de Brébeuf and Gabriel Lalemant have found a final resting place in one corner of the restored Sainte-Marie. Canadians also owe Brébeuf a debt of gratitude for his gift of the beautiful carol, "Jesus Ahatonhia," originally written in the Huron language, and beginning with the lyric that renders into English as "'Twas in the moon of wintertime/When all the birds had fled."

2. The Martyrs' Shrine, 1926
Highway 12, Midland

For the Greater Glory of God.
St. Ignatius of Loyola (1491–1556)

*I*t is almost impossible to visit Sainte-Marie-au-pays-des-Hurons without paying a complementary visit to the nearby Martyrs' Shrine. Both the construction of the Shrine and the eventual restoration of Sainte-Marie were indirect results of Father Pierre Chazzelle's visit to the area in 1844. He wrote to the Father General of the Jesuits, "May God grant that soon the ruins of Sainte-Marie be ours and profaned no more." Part of his prayer was answered in 1926 when a handsome grey stone church known as the Martyrs' Shrine was opened directly across from the original site of Sainte-Marie — to commemorate the lives of Brébeuf, Lalemant, and six other Jesuit priests (or "Canadian Martyrs") who died for their faith in the Huron–Iroquois Wars of the 1640s.

Another part of Father Chazzelle's prayer would come to life with the restoration of Sainte-Marie itself in the 1960s. As one strolls through the grounds of Sainte-Marie today, one catches a glimpse of the Martyrs' Shrine's imposing twin towers — located on a height of land that commands a view of the rolling landscape and the nearby Wye River. The interior of the Shrine is equally impressive. To remind us of Ontario's first people and their way of life, the high vaulted ceiling of narrow cedar strips is in the shape of a canoe.

One must allow time for a stroll through the grounds of the Shrine as well. Beautifully tended, the gardens are a delight. You can follow the path along the fourteen Stations of the Cross. The bronze statues are the work of the Union Artistique of Vaucouleurs, France. Beyond the Stations of the Cross is the Brébeuf Prayer Garden, and

The Martyrs' Shrine, Midland.

beyond this is a lookout with a magnificent view of Georgian Bay and the restored Sainte-Marie. The pathway winds around the Papal Visit Monument and then past the Italianate Holy Family Shrine. Before departing the Martyrs' Shrine, you can retrace your steps and descend the stairs for a visit to the Little Flower Island, and a final moment in the Prayer Gardens.

If the Jesuits of the 1640s and their Huron converts could have been present for Pope John Paul II's visit to the area in 1984, they would have marvelled to see tens of thousands of people gathered on the hillside of the Martyrs' Shrine, to watch the Pope receive the Eagle Feather, the highest honour of the Huron people. They would no doubt have sensed that their sacrifices in the destruction of Sainte-Marie so long ago had not been in vain.

For all of us today, the construction of the Martyrs' Shrine in the 1920s and the restoration of Sainte-Marie-au-pays-des-Hurons in the 1960s have ensured that the pioneering contributions of the Huron people and the missionary work of the Jesuits in seventeenth-century Ontario will not be lost to all the generations who lie ahead.

Brant County

3. St. Paul's, Her Majesty's Chapel of the Mohawks, 1785
Mohawk Street, Brantford

Ne Royaner Rownonsa Eganirwdon Ne.
Yadeyagonwenjake eh Yonnawinyontde
(The House of the Lord shall be established
and all nations shall flow into it.)
Isaiah 2:2

Overlooking the quiet waters of the Grand River, in present-day Brantford, is a small white clapboard church, much like many buildings that had begun to dot the landscape of the new province of Upper Canada, a century and a half after the destruction of Sainte-Marie. This otherwise ordinary building — erected by descendants of the old Iroquois enemies of the Huron — has a special historical significance: it is the first Protestant church built in southern Ontario.

All the lumber, which had been floated down the Grand River, was hand-hewn and the nails handcrafted. Although, over the years, much of the building has been repaired, the original siding can still be seen in a line of hand-sawing about an inch from the bottom of each board.

Because of the important historical connection between the Six Nations Iroquois and the British Crown, the singular honour of Royal Chapel was conferred on this small church in 1904. But the story of the church itself goes back another two hundred years. In 1710, during the long struggle between France and England in North America, Queen Anne provided funds for a fort and an Iroquois chapel in what is now New York State, at the junction of Schoharie Creek and the Mohawk River. Queen Anne also presented a silver communion service and a Bible to the congregation of the newly built chapel, which was named after her.

During the American Revolution (1776–1783), many among the Iroquois nation of the Mohawk remained loyal to the Crown. Finally forced to flee their homes, the followers of Joseph Brant (or Thayendanegea, war chief of the Six Nations) arrived in what is now Ontario from New York State. In recognition of their loyalty, they were granted 768,000 acres of land bordering the Grand River. Just before Brant and his followers

Her Majesty's Chapel of the Mohawks,
Brantford.

arrived, Queen Anne's Bible and silver communion service had been buried on a farm on the banks of the Mohawk River. Later they would be smuggled into Canada, and today they are still in the possession of the congregation of the Chapel of the Mohawks, on the Grand River.

The building was erected in 1785, but many alterations would take place over the ensuing years. At first, the chapel's entrance faced the Grand River; it has since been moved to the other end of the building. In 1876 a bell for the chapel was cast in London, England. In later years it was destined for the scrap heap, but public pressure came to the rescue, and the bell was placed under a small structure at the front of the chapel. A coat of arms, carved from one piece of wood and presented by George III, still hangs in the chapel. The Lord's Prayer, the Ten Commandments, and the Apostles' Creed, all in the Mohawk language, are inscribed over the altar.

More recently, eight stained glass windows depicting the history of the Six Nations in Canada have been installed. Window number one tells the story of the pre-contact period, before the arrival of people from across the sea. Denanawidah, born of a virgin during a time of strife, was an individual who was motivated by compassion. His life is symbolized by the Pine Tree of Peace, which is as sacred to the Mohawk people as the cross is to Christians. The window bears the inscription, "I am Denanawidah. I plant the great tree of peace. If any man or nation shall show a desire to obey the Great Peace, they shall be welcomed to take shelter beneath the tree. The words of Hiawatha, spokesman for Denanawidah."

Window number two reminds us of the long association between the Six Nations and the British Crown. It shows Queen Anne receiving a delegation that includes Mohawk and other members of the Iroquois Nations. Windows number three and four honour

Joseph Brant. Window number three shows him about to lead his loyal followers across Lake Ontario. In window number four Brant is welcoming the Reverend John Stuart, the first ordained minister to conduct a service in the chapel. (Brant himself died in 1807 and was initially buried in the Anglican graveyard in Burlington. In 1850 his body was removed and borne on the shoulders of young Mohawk men to its final resting place, behind the Chapel of the Mohawks.)

Window number five pictures the consecration of the chapel in 1830 by the Right Reverend James Stuart. It also reminds us of God's love and of missionary outreach to all people. Elizabeth II granted permission for the Royal Cipher to be placed in the sixth window, which is considered to be the "queen's window." Window number seven is dedicated to the education of the First Nations. The Mohawk teacher, Susan Hardy, is seen surrounded by a group of children. Window number eight displays the ascended Christ against the backdrop of a cross, with a trillium (the official flower of present-day Ontario) at the top. Another portion of the window takes the shape of a tent, symbolizing a heavenly home.

The eighth window is also said to embody a prayer that the first peoples of the country will always have an important place in the land of their ancestors. Unfortunately, in 1975 and 1976 other parts of the Chapel were damaged by fire. The Pine Tree of Peace was destroyed. Some items have been replaced. It is remarkable that this historic church remains standing after more than two hundred years. The restored Chapel is a tribute to all the First Nations of Canada.

Upper Canada
(1791–1840)

*I*n Ontario history the fifty-year period from the last decade of the eighteenth century to the fourth decade of the nineteenth is taken up by the story of the British North American province of Upper Canada — the most immediate ancestor of the Canadian province of Ontario today. The stage for this story was set by the final struggle between France and England in North America during the Seven Years War (1756–1763), and the subsequent American Revolution or War of Independence (1776–1783). The old Canadian upper country of the French and Indian fur trade, which had become part of the British empire at the end of the Seven Years War, remained within the empire at the end of the American Revolution (and so did the more northerly fur-trading territory of the Hudson's Bay Company). By the mid 1780s the old French and Indian trade had been consolidated and extended by the North West Company. North of the Great Lakes, United Empire Loyalist refugees from the former British American colonies had begun to arrive in several parts of what is now Ontario. "Upper Canada" was established in 1791 to accommodate these new English-speaking pioneers.

Though united by their desire to leave the fledgling American Republic, the Loyalists were a diverse lot. They included people of English, Irish, Scottish, German, Dutch, Aboriginal, and African descent — and Anglicans, Methodists, Presbyterians, Quakers, and Roman Catholics. They also brought with them the family-farm pioneering traditions of the Anglo-American settlement frontier, which had already begun its long westward march from the Atlantic seaboard into the heartland of the North American continent.

By the 1790s, as the modern historian of Upper Canada, Gerald Craig, has explained: "Other Americans were coming in, too, many of them Methodists, but also of other Protestant denominations .... They came to find a suitable field for their talents and energies, ready to find that field anywhere on the continent. Now it was Upper Canada, but in twenty years' time some of their kind would be as ready to move into the Mexican province of Texas, always searching for the best opportunities."

The War of 1812–14 determined that Upper Canada would have a different destiny than Texas. It also put an end to large-scale American frontier migration into the province. By the 1820s, however, still larger numbers of new settlers were arriving from Great Britain itself, across the sea. Wherever they came from and wherever they took up land, the new settlers built churches. The spiritual life of the local church in Upper Canada was a long, strong arm in a rugged and sometimes grim new environment. Happily, some of these churches remain standing today — in tribute to many now forgotten pioneer struggles of the Ontario past.

Lennox & Addington County

4. Hay Bay Church (Methodist), 1792
South Shore Road, Town of Greater Napanee

The groves were God's first temples.
Amidst the cool and silence, he knelt down
And offered to the Mightiest
Solemn thanks and supplication.

William Cullen Bryant (1794–1878)

On the shore of Hay Bay in eastern Ontario is what now qualifies as the oldest United Church building in the province. The first Methodist church to be built west of the Maritimes, Hay Bay was for many years at the centre of a vigorous brand of Christianity which, by 1900, had grown into the largest Protestant body in Canada. In 1925 the Methodists were the largest of the communions that amalgamated to form the present-day United Church of Canada.

Many years before, on an exceedingly severe day in the winter of 1790, a woman looked through the rough-hewn window of her St. Lawrence River home and saw a lone figure on horseback. With snow swirling all around, a one-armed man struggled from the back of his horse and, rapping on the door, asked for shelter. William Losee had arrived in Upper Canada to begin his pioneer Methodist ministry.

In February 1791 Losee formed what was called the Bay of Quinte Circuit. Although not the first Methodist in Upper Canada, he is regarded by many as the founder of Methodism in what is now called Ontario. He was not an ordained minister, but a deacon who would one day be admitted, on trial, into full connection. This permitted him to use the title "Reverend," and to baptize the faithful. Two years of further progress through the ranks would have allowed him to become an elder, after which he could also perform marriages and administer the sacraments. Perhaps because of an unrequited love affair, he never quite made the grade.

A compelling speaker, Losee soon had a large following. One of many early circuit riders or saddle-bag preachers, he rode on horseback from village to village spreading the word of God. In the early days of their ministry, these dedicated preachers knocked on doors and delivered their sermons to whoever was present. This earned them yet another nickname: "thunderers at the door." It was this kind of zeal that created a swell of converts to Methodism in Upper Canada.

With the rapid growth of the denomination in the Bay of Quinte region, the erection of a permanent place of worship became a high priority. It is believed that the building of the Hay Bay Church began around 1792. Most early churches of this sort were built by the joint labour of the community. The men felled the trees, squared the timber, and drew it to the designated place. Willing hands framed the building. The usual practice was to hold a bee to enclose the frame, lay the floor, and roof the edifice. As soon as this stage was reached, the congregation, seated on rough planks, would begin their prayer meetings. When finances permitted, the interiors would be finished and furnishings provided. Usually this would take a number of years.

Hay Bay Church, like many pioneer institutions, had its own personal tragedy. On Sunday, August 29, 1819, the congregation was engaged in a prayer meeting. As the words "it might be a day long to be remembered" sounded through the primitive chapel, screams of distress were heard coming from the Bay. Intending to attend service, eighteen young people had set out from the north shore in a boat that began leaking halfway into their voyage. Just three hundred yards from the south shore, the boat rapidly filled

The old Hay Bay Methodist Church, Napanee.

and sank in a few feet of water. In spite of valiant efforts to save the young people, nine were drowned. On the Monday following the tragedy, the bodies of seven young ladies and two young men were interred in the pioneer cemetery across the dirt road from the Hay Bay Church.

After his long commitment to Methodism in Upper Canada, the aging William Losee returned to his former home on Long Island, New York. The years of horseback riding on wilderness trails through the bitter cold of winter and the heat of summer had taken their toll. Losee died on October 16, 1832, and was buried in the cemetery of Hemstead Methodist Episcopal — his boyhood church. Fifteen months later, his wife, Mary, was laid by his side.

For years the centre of a vigorous religious life, the old Hay Bay Church eventually outlived its usefulness, and embarked on a period of turbulent existence. Even in its heyday it had sometimes been used as a court house, and it served as a military barracks during the War of 1812–14. In the later nineteenth century, it would suffer the indignity of being used as a storage place for animal fodder, and ultimately as a sheepfold.

In 1910, through the efforts of concerned citizens, the old Hay Bay Church building was repossessed by the Methodist Church and the work of restoration began. The interior was refurbished in the same style as the original. The very high pulpit had a commanding view of the congregation's plain wooden benches. On August 21, 1912, the official re-opening of the restored church took place. In 1925, when church union occurred, the Hay Bay Church became the property of the United Church of Canada, which continues to care for the building today.

In 1969, through the action of the Committee on Archives of the United Church of Canada, the headstones of William Losee and his wife, Mary, which had fallen and were about to be replaced on Long Island, were brought to Canada. They were erected in a suitable cairn in the cemetery across the road from the Hay Bay Church.

In 1892 the Methodist clergyman, Richard Duke, had written, "Any thing that perpetuates the memory of a special providence is worth preserving. This old Hay Bay Church links us visibly with the rise of Methodism in Ontario; it is, so to speak, a visible embodiment of a hundred years of our history as a distinct people in this land." More than a century later, commemorative services are still being held.

York Region

5. Quaker Meeting House, 1810
Yonge Street, Newmarket

Where two or three are gathered together in
my name, there am I in the midst of them.
Matthew 18:20

In 1801 one Timothy Rogers came to the Newmarket area in the central part of Upper Canada, in search of lands for forty Quaker families who wished to leave the new American Republic. Rogers was a member of the Society of Friends, a religious movement that had sprung up in the Lake District of England during the turbulent seventeenth century. Rooted in inward spiritual awareness and veracity, the movement was founded by George Fox.

Quakerism is based on a religious way of life rather than an accepted dogma. The Friends consider themselves neither Catholic nor Protestant. They favour a "third way" of Christianity, emphasizing fundamental differences from Roman Catholic authority, hierarchy, and absolute creed. Unlike Protestant denominations, which stress particular interpretations as found in the Holy Bible, the Society of Friends also emphasizes religion as a fellowship of the spirit. Essentials of Quaker unity are the love of God and the love of people, conceived and practiced in the spirit of Jesus Christ. The basis of the religious fellowship is an inward, personal experience. Christian qualities matter much more than Christian dogma. Although the Bible is central to the Friends, they seek to find truth in its pages, rather than accepting what is written as dictated. The faith of the Friends rests on absolute sincerity. God is experienced through the Inward Light which is the Spirit of Christ within. Dean W.R. Inge described Quakerism as having remained the nearest of all Christian bodies to the example of Christ.

When Timothy Rogers' group of Quakers arrived in the Newmarket area in the early nineteenth century, they were given two years to cultivate and fence ten acres of their land. They were also required to clear thirty-five feet in front of their property, half of which was to become part of a public road. (In this case the road was the present-day

Quaker Meeting House, Newmarket.

Yonge Street, which would subsequently develop into what is claimed to be the longest street in the world.)

In 1804 the senior Philadelphia branch of the Friends in the United States granted the small group in Newmarket, Upper Canada, the right of a Preparative Meeting. As many other early settlers had to do, the Newmarket Quakers at first met in their homes for worship. Then in 1810 one of the settlers, William Doan, donated two acres of land on Lot 92, Concession 1W, Yonge Street, for a meeting house. The earliest such structure for Christian religious purposes north of the Town of York, the board-and-batten construction was so sound that, over the years, the building has remained virtually unaltered. A sliding partition divides the interior down the centre. Two sets of doors provide separate entrances for men and women.

The Friends' form of service is without prearranged character or formalized program. They have no ritual, no ordained pastor, and no outward sacraments. Reminiscent of the theology of Martin Luther, God can be approached by the individual without any intermediary priest or preacher. Quaker meeting houses are simple buildings, without steeples, stained-glass windows, altars, or organs. Silent worship is often presented as the most distinctive Quaker practice. The Friends gather at an appointed time. They rise to speak or kneel to pray spontaneously. After an hour of such worship the meeting breaks up, and everyone shakes hands with the neighbours sitting on either side. Regular

Sunday morning services are still held in the Newmarket Meeting House.

Immediately to the south of the simple building is the unusual early graveyard of the Newmarket Quaker settlement. Marking the deep commitment and dedication of the original religious community, the settlers are buried in order of the date of their deaths rather than in family plots. Family names are scattered throughout the cemetery.

6. Sharon Temple, 1825
18974 Leslie Street, Sharon, Town of East Gwillimbury

> *The new church or chapel of the Children of Peace is certainly calculated to inspire the beholder with astonishment; its dimensions — its architecture — its situation — are all so extraordinary.*
> William Lyon Mackenzie (1795–1861)

*E*ven today the Sharon Temple, not far from the old Quaker Meeting House in Newmarket, is one of Ontario's most unusual buildings. At first sight, the square structure conjures up a vision of a wedding cake. Built between 1825 and 1831, this amazing architectural achievement was the dream of David Willson, the founder of a religious group known as the Children of Peace.

Willson was born in 1778, in Duchess County, New York, of Irish parents. Very young when his father died, he was almost literally uneducated, his schooling limited to less than one year. For some time he earned his living by working on ocean-going vessels. This profession was not to his liking, however, and he decided to move with his wife and children to Upper Canada, where the family settled in the Township of East Gwillimbury.

A deeply religious man, David Willson at first joined the Society of Friends in the Newmarket area, but his active participation was of short duration. He entertained some rather unorthodox ideas that did not please his Quaker colleagues: he actually enjoyed music and he did not see how conforming to a particular dress style had much to do with religion. The Society of Friends dismissed him from their circle. Not particularly perturbed, and accompanied by some more liberal-minded Friends, he started The Children of Peace.

Adherents of this new group were free to enjoy their music. Immediately, both singing voices and musical instruments were introduced into their worship services. They organized a brass band that was considered one of the finest of its kind. Their numbers grew, and soon enough they required a place larger than their original small log building. A forty-foot-square meeting house was built to accommodate the growing congregation.

This new meeting house, however, was still not enough for David Willson. He had a dream. He wanted to erect his idea of the perfect temple — which would symbolize the Holy Trinity. The result of this dream is the three-storey edifice that still stands in the old village of Sharon, rising seventy-five feet in height. Like Solomon's Temple in the Old Testament, this remarkable structure took seven years to build.

The ground floor is sixty feet square — and proclaims that members of The Children

Sharon Temple, East Gwillimbury.

of Peace intended to deal squarely with all people. Each side has a large door so that whoever came into the temple entered on an equal footing. Equal numbers of windows on each side, with a total of 2952 panes of glass, allow the light of the Gospel to shine on all within the Temple. When the building was finally completed a special service was held, on the evening of the first Friday in September, 1831. With candles blazing in every window, the event must have presented an enchanting spectacle to passersby.

Twelve pillars symbolizing the twelve apostles support the upper storeys. This theme was repeated by placing a spire containing a lantern on each corner of the three-storey structure. A gilded ball on the top storey seems to float above the Temple. In order to send a message to the world, the word "Peace" is inscribed on the ball. Inside, a fragile, metal staircase with no handrail soars to a second-storey gallery. Before the congregation entered, members of the choir and band would wend their way up this perilous staircase to the second storey. From there music would waft over the congregation as they entered the Temple.

The third floor, a simple square, is open to the ground floor below. In the centre of the Temple is the Ark which stands on twelve gilded pillars, again representing the twelve apostles. The Ark, like the Temple, is square. It took 365 days to complete, and contains the Bible. The four pillars at each corner of the Ark are inscribed with the words of the four cardinal virtues: Faith, Hope, Love, and Charity. The Temple also houses one of the oldest barrel organs in the province. Built in 1820 by Richard Coates, it still functions today and a visitor may be favoured with a selection of its tunes.

For reasons known only to David Willson, services were held on three special days of the year, and on the last Saturday of each month when members made contributions for charitable purposes. Willson himself was the only pastor to minister to the congregation. His dedicated flock passed their lives in helping each other and the poor around them. When, at the age of 87, Willson passed on to his reward in the hereafter, the group began to fall in numbers. Eventually, The Children of Peace became extinct. Yet David Willson's magnificent temple remains today as a museum — and a beautiful monument to a man who had a dream.

Glengarry County

7. St. Andrew's United Church, 1818
Williamstown

From the lone shieling of the misty island
Mountains divide us, and the waste of sea.
Yet still the blood is strong, the heart is Highland,
And we in dreams behold the Hebrides.
"The Skye Boat Song"

*B*orn on the Isle of Skye and educated at King's College, Aberdeen, the Reverend John Bethune was the first minister of the Kirk of Scotland to come to Upper Canada. After his ordination he had served in North Carolina as chaplain to the Royal Highland Emigrant Regiment. Imprisoned during the American Revolution, he was later exchanged as a prisoner of war. When peace was declared he moved to Glengarry County, where he founded the new province's first Presbyterian church in present-day Williamstown. Soon enough, he had established a number of other churches in the area as well.

The Reverend John Bethune is also remembered as the great-great-grandfather of Dr. Norman Bethune, the Canadian surgeon so revered by the Chinese people in the twentieth century. Unfortunately, the Reverend Bethune, now often said to be the father of Presbyterianism in Upper Canada, did not live to see the completion of the present St. Andrew's Church in Williamstown, which dates from 1818. His death in 1815 was attributed to illness resulting from his earlier incarceration as a prisoner of war.

The original Presbyterian church that Bethune established in 1787 was a primitive log structure, with plank seats resting on cedar blocks, and also served as a school. This was replaced in 1804 by a structure built of stone which, unfortunately, caved in on itself and collapsed during a very heavy snowfall in 1809. The bell from this structure, however (a gift from the fur trader, Sir Alexander Mackenzie — who had written "From Canada By Land" on a rock at the edge of the Pacific Ocean), was rescued and is still in use in the present building.

Rebuilding began in 1812 and was completed in 1818. Both French Canadian and English influences are apparent in St. Andrew's as we see it now. French Canadian

masons gave the church its Québécois appearance — with its high walls and an octagonal belfry on a small pyramidal roof, topped by a jaunty rooster or chanticleer. The windows with their elaborate Palladian motif reflect an English influence. The massive
decorative truss and porch at the main entrance were added in the 1870s.

The original interior was furnished in the style of St. Nicholas East Kirk in Aberdeen.
The square pews were allocated by lot, each member contributing twenty pounds to
secure a deed to a pew. The minister's family, the elders, and six partners of the fur-trading North West Company were given priority seats. In order to receive communion, each
member was expected to participate in a preparatory service. Those who qualified would
then receive a pewter token which would be presented on Communion Sunday. The

St Andrew's United Church, Williamstown.

custom continued even after
St. Andrew's became a
United Church in 1925, and
was still observed in recent
times.

In the early twentieth
century the congregation
decided to modernize the
interior. The old-fashioned
square pews, with their
squeaking doors, and the
high forbidding pulpit were
removed. The inside of the
church was transformed into
the present pleasing place of
worship. Scottish ancestry,
however, is still evident in
the decorations: the cross of
St. Andrew and the emblem
of Scotland, the thistle,
grace the banner hanging
near the altar.

Back in the early nine-
teenth century the land on
which the church was built
had been sold at one point
to the great fur trader and

map maker, David Thompson, by the Reverend Bethune's widow. Not wishing to have a church and a cemetery on his hands, Thompson returned it to the congregation for the sum of twenty-five pounds.

Today, inside a wrought-iron fence, a very historic Canadian cemetery surrounds the field stone church. A walk through the quiet grounds reveals the names of many memorable people — especially retired partners of the North West Company ("the forerunner of the present confederation in Canada," as a famous historian has said). Erected by his six sons, the memorial stone of the Reverend John Bethune is located in a beautiful tree-shaded spot.

Many of the early Scottish settlers who worshiped at St. Andrew's must have had feelings like those of the anonymous poet of "The Skye Boat Song," who wrote so eloquently about his longing for the Hebrides homeland. Most of them knew they would never see their birthplace again. They had left behind relatives and friends, and ventured into an unknown country. They were now and forever part of a new world.

Leaving through the front gate today, one must pause to read the plaque dedicated to the hardy Upper Canadian pioneers who would have such a great influence on the future province of Ontario. The same tribute can be paid to all who went before, and all who followed after — in the new country of Canada that the fur trade had done so much to bring together:

> *Tread softly, stranger,*
> *Reverently draw near,*
> *The Vanguard of a*
> *Nation slumbers here.*

8. St. Raphaels Roman Catholic Church, 1821
St. Raphaels, south of Alexandria

9. St. Mary's Roman Catholic Church, 1849
Williamstown

> *Fair these broad meads — these hoary woods are grand;*
> *But we are exiles from our fathers' land.*
> "The Skye Boat Song"

During the late eighteenth and early nineteenth centuries, Roman Catholics as well as Presbyterians with roots in the Scottish Highlands arrived in Glengarry County, in the most easterly part of Upper Canada. Some arrived at the time of the Loyalist migrations in the 1780s. Others came when disbanded Highland troops from across the sea moved to the area in 1804, accompanied by their chaplain, Father Alexander Macdonnell. There were also Scottish Catholics among the North West Company fur traders who settled in the county.

During the War of 1812–14, Father Macdonnell rallied his Scottish Highland veterans to form the 2nd Glengarry Fencible Regiment, and went into action with them

The ruins of St. Raphaels Roman Catholic Church.

against the Americans. (As the original Glengarry Fencibles back in the old country, many of the same men had fought for the British Crown in Ireland. This demonstration of loyalty helped secure a position of influence for Macdonnell, and a more secure place for Roman Catholicism in a new British North American province that had quickly acquired and would long maintain a strong Protestant majority. Macdonnell would go on to serve on the provincial Legislative Council, and ultimately become the first Roman Catholic Bishop of Upper Canada.

For a time after the War of 1812–14 the most important Roman Catholic church in Upper Canada was St. Raphaels in Glengarry County, completed in 1821. Fourteen of the sixty-nine original members of

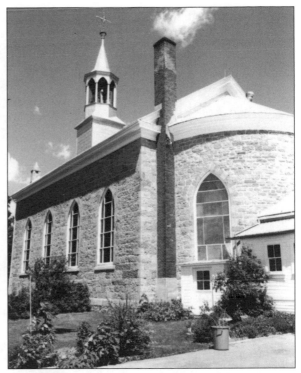

St Mary's Roman Catholic Church, Williamstown.

the church were partners in the North West Company ("the first organization to operate on a continental scale in North America"). Built on an impressive scale itself, St. Raphaels established a precedent for other Roman Catholic churches in the province. Then, when both the episcopal see and Bishop Macdonnell subsequently moved to Kingston, St. Raphaels became a grand church in a small rural parish, with some unique memories of the Ontario past.

Regrettably, a fire destroyed most of the church in 1970: only the bare stone walls remained. Capping of the exposed tops of the walls and stabilization of the ruins were carried out by the Ontario Heritage Foundation. Ownership then passed into the hands of the Mission of Friends of the Ruins of St. Raphaels, who still sometimes hold open-air concerts inside the walls during the summer season.

Until 1854, St. Mary's Church in nearby Williamstown was part of the St. Raphaels Mission. Begun in 1847, it was completed in 1849. Perhaps the most fascinating feature of this church is its ceiling. St. Mary's was completely renovated and redecorated in 1916. Canvasses representing religious mysteries were painted in New York and applied to the vaulted ceiling. When gazing up at the beautiful frescoes, you feel you are looking at a miniature of the Sistine Chapel in Rome.

Following Vatican II, many Catholic churches had their reredos removed; fortunately St. Mary's retained theirs, along with the beautiful statue of the Immaculate Conception behind the main altar. Purchased in France, the Stations of the Cross are oil paintings. Some of the stained glass windows commemorate the martyrdom of Fathers Brébeuf and Lalemant.

For too long in Ontario's earlier history, relations among Christian denominations were often characterized by contempt rather than love. Although all denominations faced similar problems in their new environment, interdenominational associations were few. But St. Mary's Roman Catholic Church and St.

St. Mary's main altar.

Andrew's Presbyterian (now United) Church in Williamstown were different — a model of ecumenism from the start. Their long history of co-operation and fellowship culminated in 1980, when the clergy of both congregations assisted in the dedication of St. Andrew's as a Loyalist Church.

Niagara Region

10. St. Andrew's Presbyterian Church, 1831
323 Simcoe Street, Niagara-on-the-Lake

> And they shall beat their swords into plow-
> shares and their spears into pruning hooks:
> nation shall not lift up a sword against
> nation, neither shall they learn war anymore.
>
> Micah 4:3

The impressive stone fort that still stands on what is now the American side of the Niagara River, where the river meets Lake Ontario, has origins that stretch back to the early days of the Canadian fur trade under the French regime, in 1676. But "Fort Niagara" had finally fallen into British hands during the summer of 1759. Some two decades later in the 1780s, in the company of several hundred Butler's Rangers, various United Empire Loyalist refugees from the American Revolution began to cluster around both sides of the river. This led to the Loyalist pioneer settlements that established present-day Niagara-on-the-Lake, Ontario.

The place was originally called Newark by Lieutenant Governor John Graves Simcoe, and served briefly as the capital of the new province of Upper Canada. (The forces of the British empire did not finally surrender the fort on the other side of the river to the new American republic until 1796.) Scottish Presbyterian merchants played an important role in the early life of Simcoe's Newark, and the first Protestant church in Newark, begun in 1794, was Presbyterian. Hoping to see the Church of England established as the official religion of the new province, Lieutenant Governor Simcoe was not pleased.

In August 1813, during the War of 1812–14, Newark was occupied by American troops. Because they feared the British could use the Presbyterian church as a lookout and signal tower, the troops torched the building, reducing it to a pile of ashes. Before the year was out, American forces set the town alight, causing the inhabitants to flee into the snow-filled streets. The Reverend Robert Addison, minister of the Presbyterian church, was taken prisoner and interned until the end of the war.

After the destruction of their church, it would be eighteen years before the local

Presbyterians erected another. The foundation stone of the present-day St. Andrew's Church in Niagara-on-the-Lake was dedicated in May 1831. Although invading forces no longer posed a threat to the community, the church was now besieged by natural phenomena. A series of hurricanes ripped through the area in the 1830s and seemed to single out St. Andrew's as their victim. In 1855 one particularly violent storm hurled the Gabriel figure that graced the steeple to the ground and caused extensive damage to the roof and the interior. Lightning caused a fire that damaged the upper portion of the building. Architect Kivas Tully was engaged to repair the damage and, after considerable work, the church was restored. A new bell was hung in the belfry to call the faithful to prayer. Then once again, in 1950, the church was threatened by fire. Ignited by a welder's torch, the blaze was

St Andrew's Presbyterian Church, Niagara-on-the-Lake.

confined to the tower, which was reduced to a skeleton. Finally, in 1991, major renovations were undertaken, to restore both exterior and interior as they were when the church was built in 1831.

Today's architectural gem may be one of the few churches in Ontario where there is no hint of Gothic design. With its Doric portico, Classical facade, Georgian shell, and simple octagonal steeple, it is indeed an eclectic structure. Its three-sided gallery overlooking the straight-backed box pews with their panelled doors, and its spacious rectangular interior, reflect the Presbyterian heritage of its people. From the lofty pulpit, surmounted by a golden dove, the minister looks down on his congregation. Because the pulpit is situated just inside the entrance, no bride gets to walk down the traditional aisle. Instead, she must enter through one of the doors that flank the pulpit, circle around the back of the pews, and move up the other side, into the railed communion area in front of the precentor's desk.

Visiting this unique house of worship today is a trip backward in time. On Communion Sunday one can sit in a box pew and partake of Holy Communion from the same silver service that was used in 1831. Standing in the lofty pulpit, the minister, God's representative, still delivers his message to the congregation from a place on high.

11. Drummond Hill Presbyterian Church, 1836
6136 Lundy's Lane, Niagara Falls

To the south of Niagara-on-the-Lake, on the highest spot between Lakes Erie and Ontario, is Lundy's Lane, site of the present-day Drummond Hill Presbyterian Church. The original church, a low frame building painted red, stood about a hundred yards from the site of one of the bloodiest modern battles ever fought on Canadian soil. On July 25, 1814, in the quiet country lane of William Lundy, a decisive battle of the War of 1812–14 took place.

During the earlier part of July 1814, American troops had captured Fort Erie and defeated the British at Chippawa (in the present-day city of Niagara Falls, Ontario), but failed to take Fort George, on the opposite side of the river from the old Fort Niagara. While retiring to a safer area, they were forced to defend themselves on the high ridge of land at Lundy's Lane. Starting around six o'clock on the sultry summer evening of July 25, the battle raged on until after midnight. One thousand British, Canadian, and Indian allies, later joined by twelve hundred reinforcements, fought against five thousand American troops. During the fierce encounter, much of it hand-to-hand combat at bayonet point, the British, Canadians, and Indians suffered close to a thousand casualties, while the Americans lost one-third of their number. The battle was a stalemate, but the forces of the British empire remained in possession of the hill.

It was left to the British forces to bury the dead, friend and foe alike. Those who weren't cremated on an immense pyre made of fence posts were buried in trenches. Tradition holds that, for many years, no grass grew on the site of the cremation. The little red church had been in the midst of the fray. In a diary account one survivor of the battle wrote, "We fought in and through the Presbyterian church on the hill and left it a shambles." In 1819 a second church was built on the far side of a cemetery that can still be visited.

Wandering through the cemetery today, one finds the gravesite of Laura Secord, Canada's own heroine of the War of 1812–14. The daughter of a United Empire Loyalist, she had arrived in Upper Canada in 1795. By the time the war broke out, Laura was married with five children.

During the Battle of Queenston Heights, the Secord home was in the direct line of fire. Laura and her children raced to safety. After the battle was over, Laura's first act of heroism was to search the battlefield for her badly wounded husband, a sergeant in the 1st Lincoln Militia. When they returned to their home they found that it had been looted.

Later in the war, American soldiers were billeted in the Secord house. When Laura overheard their plan of attack, she set out on foot on a twenty-mile journey. Evading the American troops, she travelled through tangled woods and insect-infested swamps. Although the story that a cow accompanied her may be fiction, her courage and daring cannot be questioned. As a result of

Laura Secord's Monument in the Drummond Hill Cemetery, Niagara Falls.

information she gave to Lieutenant FitzGibbon, the Americans walked into an ambush at what later became known as the Battle of Beaver Dams, a turning point in the war. Many years later, in 1860, the Prince of Wales, on a tour of Canada, rewarded an older Laura Secord with one hundred pounds for her services to the British Crown.

In the years following the War of 1812–14, the battlefield at Lundy's Lane became an early tourist attraction. In 1836 a new brick Presbyterian Church was built on the battlefield. From that vantage point, the lines of trenches and burial places could be seen.

Today old record books, with the signatures of thousands of visitors, bear silent testimony to the popularity of this historic site in an earlier era. Subsequently, the site lapsed as an attraction, and a wilderness of vines and bushes became the silent guardians of the lonely battlefield.

It wasn't until 1887, when the founder of the Lundy's Lane Historical Society, Canon George Bull, took an interest that an attempt was made to restore the site. More years would pass before a monument was erected. In 1895, a granite shaft, forty feet high on a twenty-foot-square base was unveiled. Soldiers' bones, recovered from the battle site, were entombed in the vault below the monument. Over the years, during construction in the area, bones of soldiers of the Battle of Lundy's Lane have been found. These remains have typically been buried in the cemetery as well, with appropriate military honours.

In 1901 a special monument was erected over Laura Secord's grave, replacing her original headstone. A bronze bust of the brave heroine who played such a strong role in bringing about victory at Beaver Dams surmounts the monument.

The Lundy's Lane Historical Society held a ceremony on July 25, 1964, the 150th anniversary of the Battle of Lundy's Lane in the War of 1812–14. Both Canadian and American flags were placed on the graves, to celebrate 150 years of ensuing peace between the two nations. Flags of the "176th Battalion C.E.F. Niagara Rangers" hang on the walls of the Drummond Hill Presbyterian Church today. The main window, which depicts Moses standing barefoot at the Burning Bush, is best seen at night from across the street. Drummond Hill Presbyterian still stands guard over Lundy's Lane and the adjoining cemetery. A visit to the place pays tribute to those brave men who fought and died to ensure a unique Canadian future.

Kent County
(Municipality of Chatham-Kent)

12. British Methodist Episcopal Church, 1834
Uncle Tom's Cabin Museum, Dresden

> *When we let freedom ring ... When all of God's*
> *children will be able to join hands and sing in the*
> *words of the old Negro Spiritual, "Free at last! Free*
> *at last! Thank God Almighty, we are free at last."*
> Martin Luther King, Jr. (1929–1968)

*I*n the first half of the nineteenth century, before the American Civil War, the unique British North American province of Upper Canada became a haven for some 30,000 to 40,000 African American refugees from the United States. To escape the unbearable bonds of slavery, Black Americans flocked in particular to the southwestern part of the province via the Underground Railroad — a system of secret routes and safe houses used to spirit the fugitives through hostile states. Where they settled, around such places as Buxton, Chatham, Windsor, and Amherstburg, they built churches.

The New Dawn Settlement in present-day Dresden is one of the best known of these Black Ontario pioneer communities. Its most famous personality was rowed across the Niagara River from Buffalo to Fort Erie on the Canadian shore in 1830. Josiah Henson (or Uncle Tom, as some say), was born on June 15, 1789, at Charles County, Maryland. His mother taught him the Lord's Prayer and as much knowledge of religion as an uneducated slave woman could know. Although slaves were not allowed inside the plantation church, Josiah stood outside to listen to the sermon. His ear caught the message that Christ had come for all men, even those in chains.

Later, when Josiah's new master became embroiled in a brawl and was severely beaten, Josiah dragged him from the tavern. So incensed that a mere slave dared to intervene, several overseers waylaid the unfortunate Josiah and beat him so badly that his shoulder blades were broken. The bones knitted but he never regained full use of his arms.

A conscientious worker, Josiah was put in charge of selling his master's farm produce at local markets. There he mingled with gentlemen, absorbing the words and phrases that

British Methodist Episcopal Church, Dresden.

he heard them utter. During this time he began preaching to both fellow slaves and, eventually, a mixed congregation, and he was accepted as a preacher in the Methodist Episcopal Church.

When Josiah was able to raise the money to buy his freedom, his rascally master tricked him by writing into his certificate of freedom double the price agreed upon. The illiterate slave put his X on the document, condemning himself to a further life of slavery. When he learned that his master intended to sell him, he became terrified of being sent down river to Alabama (a fate worse than death itself), and began to plan his escape. On a moonlit night in September 1830, a fellow slave rowed

Uncle Tom's Cabin Museum, Dresden.

Josiah, his wife, and four children across the Ohio River to Indiana. There, Henson persuaded a sympathetic river boat captain that he would work hard for free passage to Buffalo, where he and his family could cross the Niagara River to Canada and freedom.

With some help from his Quaker friend, James C. Fuller, Henson was eventually able to establish a Black colony at Dawn, Upper Canada, later known as Dresden. The community built a sawmill, a blacksmith shop, a carpentry shop, and other facilities to help prepare former slaves to make their way in a free country. Much time was spent in the newly built school, learning to read and write, and in a small church where Reverend Henson preached God's message of hope. The colony flourished and became a fountainhead of Black Christianity in Upper Canada.

Josiah himself became prominent beyond the borders of the New Dawn Settlement. At his peril, he made journeys deep into the slave states to help others escape. During one of these trips Harriet Beecher Stowe invited him to her home in Andover, Massachusetts. It is claimed that from this meeting Mrs. Stowe acquired much of the material for her famous book, *Uncle Tom's Cabin*, and she herself wrote that the "real history of Josiah Henson, in some ways, goes even beyond that of Uncle Tom in traits of heroic manhood."

Reverend Henson also made several trips to Britain in order to raise money for his settlement in Upper Canada. On his third trip, he was received by Queen Victoria. A man who had been born into the unenviable state of slavery had reached the enviable position of shaking hands with a queen. His remaining days were spent on his farm near Dresden, where on May 5, 1883, at ninety-four years of age, he was laid to rest in a plot on his own land.

Today this farm property is the site of the Dresden Museum, which contains a collection of rare books pertaining to the abolitionist era, and other memorabilia relating to the life of the Reverend Josiah Henson. To remind the world of human cruelty towards fellow humans, the museum displays the whips, handcuffs, ball and chain, and other pitiless devices used to keep the Black slaves of America under control. In the charming board-and-batten church, weathered by the intervening years, is the pulpit from which Josiah Henson preached to his flock. One has only to stand in front of the church to visualize the many footsteps that, over the years, tamped the earthen path leading to the open door.

Simcoe County

13. St. James-on-the-Lines Church (Anglican), 1836
Church Street, Penetanguishene

> This is my commandment,
> That ye shall love one another.
> John 15:12

*A*ny account of pioneering in Upper Canada would be incomplete without some mention of the important contribution that the military forces of the British empire made to the life of the new province. (One present-day historian has even described Upper Canada as "A Military Colony in the Wilderness.") Perhaps nothing exemplifies this better than the Old Garrison Church erected on the Penetanguishene military reserve in the later 1830s.

The unusual name of St. James-on-the-Lines seems to refer to the lines of communication or the military roads that strategically linked the British naval and military establishment at Penetanguishene, on Georgian Bay, with Fort York in Toronto, on Lake Ontario. Work on the Penetanguishene establishment had begun after the War of 1812–14, with a view to future contests of the same sort that never happened. It finally brought to life one of Lieutenant Governor Simcoe's still earlier visions for the defence of the province, itself inspired by an ancient fur trade transportation corridor (which lives on today as Highway 400).

Church attendance was a must for the military men of the day. Always faced with the prospect of their immediate demise, soldiers, in order to keep their souls in good condition, were regularly marched to church. The still quite youthful province's official elite was still hoping that the Church of England would become the official religion of Upper Canada, and St. James-on-the-Lines on the old Penetanguishene military reserve is still an Anglican church today. In its heyday it was a spiritual guide to such defenders of the empire as The Royal Berkshires and the Hindustan Regiment. Funds to build the church were obtained largely through the exertions of the local naval commandant, Captain John Moberly, R.N.

As one approaches the church today, one is aware of what looks like a stone throne to the left of the doorway. There is apparently no explanation of why it was brought to this location from a local property, but it does add some special interest. Seated upon it, one can experience a few moments of quiet meditation. One can also notice how large, hand-wrought iron hinges support the heavy double doors that gave marching regiments, four abreast, ready access to the wide-aisled interior of the building.

During their leisure time, enlisted men were assigned the task of carving the pews, resulting in a variety of styles. The officers' pews at the front, with detailed carving on the end boards, are slightly more ornate than the rest. The unique military-style reredo was carved by a relative of the first rector. It is said that the carver was ill with tuberculosis and, in order to get the job completed before he died, he lived in the church.

Although the soldiers of the empire always faced the possibility of death in battle, they were sometimes a more immediate danger to themselves. Young and bored, the men of the Penetanguishene naval and military establishment frequented the neighbouring town. On one occasion, a young officer, on his way back to the barracks, fell from a horse-drawn cutter and froze to death. A double memorial tablet in the church records

St. James-on-the-Lines Anglican Church, Penetanguishene.

the event. The young officer's companion, a fellow officer, contracted pneumonia and was expected to die as well. Luckily, he recovered and was posted elsewhere. The blank side of the stone was never filled in: one might say it remains in memory of the one who got away.

Local legend has it that several military buildings in the area are haunted. The spirits of ghostly soldiers are said to parade in and around the "old British fort." Many people have apparently experienced strange phenomena in the vicinity of the place. It would be easy enough to believe that a ghostly horde of red-coated military personnel still march four abreast down the aisle of St. James-on-the-Lines on a dark and wintry Sunday morning.

An interesting brass memorial tablet was placed in the chancel by the first rector of the parish, in memory of his wife. Many years later, when the rector passed to his own reward, another inscription was added to the tablet: "In memory of George Hallen ... who for thirty-six years served the Garrison Church ... born on the 15th day of February, 1974, he fell asleep in the Lord on the 3rd day of September, 1882." This inconsistency in his birth date is evidence that you can't believe everything you read, even when it's carved in brass.

A walk through the quaint adjoining cemetery today reveals some interesting epitaphs, one of which attests to some early spirit of ecumenism. Afraid of contracting diphtheria, no pallbearers of the Protestant persuasion could be recruited for a child who had succumbed to the disease. Local Roman Catholic volunteers nonetheless willingly carried the body to its grave, and the moss-encrusted stone bears the following epitaph:

> Dear Brother, o'er your body here I weep,
> One week after with you I sleep.
> Four kind Papists here me laid,
> The Rev. G.H. the service read.

Along with both the child and the Reverend George Hallen, many local community pioneers and military leaders from the Penetanguishene area are also buried in the cemetery. They still bear witness to the role of the soldiers of the empire in the growth of Upper Canada.

14. St. Thomas Anglican Church, 1838
Shanty Bay, near Barrie

Where undisturbed for centuries of time
The opalescent waters of the lake
Have lapped the shores, full twenty leagues apart.
Sir Gerald Dodson (1884–1966)

*W*hen Mary Gapper arrived in Upper Canada in the fall of 1828, it was only supposed to be for a short visit. She had disembarked from the ship that brought her across the ocean in New York City, and was soon writing the journals that would help provide future generations with a detailed picture of life in the new land. Resigned to a life of spinsterhood, she fully intended to return to England to resume her teaching duties. While staying with her brother in the Thornhill area north of what was then called the Town of York (now Toronto), however, Mary was introduced to a veteran of the Napoleonic Wars. Newly arrived in Upper Canada, Lieutenant Colonel Edward O'Brien became a frequent visitor to the Gapper establishment in Thornhill. In order to become Mrs. O'Brien, Mary relinquished her plans to return to the land of her birth.

Colonel O'Brien had been appointed government agent, in charge of settling Black American immigrants in Oro Township, in Simcoe County. The newlyweds moved from Thornhill to Kempenfelt Bay, about six miles from the then quite small settlement at Barrie. Here they cleared the first lot and built the first log house in the area. In her journal, Mary called their new dwelling a Canadian shanty. Hollowed-out troughs of basswood trees, laid side by side and covered with other such logs turned the other way,

St. Thomas Church, Shanty Bay.

45

Dockside Service, St. Thomas Church, Shanty Bay.

formed the roof — slanted front to back above the crude log walls. Soon enough the O'Briens replaced their shanty with a larger, two-storey log house, which they named "The Woods." This became the nucleus of a small settlement of semi-retired or "half-pay" personnel from the British army. Other Canadian shanties sprang up, and Mary O'Brien promptly assigned the name Shanty Bay to the new community.

Her journals gives us a glimpse of the life and times of these particular Upper Canadian settlers. Mary describes how a team of oxen, which were being brought across the frozen Bay, broke through the ice. All capable hands rushed some two miles across the ice to rescue the driver, who had been unable to keep the animals from sinking. Although exhausted from their successful rescue, they assembled that evening for their customary daily prayer.

The community of Shanty Bay grew slowly, and the burden of building a church would rest on the shoulders of a few determined people. The project became a prime concern for the O'Briens. Although they were better off financially than many British immigrants to Upper Canada, funds were still scarce. In her journal, Mrs. O'Brien records that her husband would "build the church with what assistance he can get according to his own notion."

Like many others in the new province, the O'Briens would model their new church after one from their past. The design of St. Thomas at Shanty Bay was copied from a church in County Clare, Ireland. Almost twenty years elapsed before the church was completed and consecrated. Colonel O'Brien used a building method called "rammed earth" or "cob." A mixture of chopped straw and wet clay were trampled by oxen, and then rammed into wooden forms. As with concrete, once the material set, the forms were removed. Placed on a massive stone foundation, the three-foot-thick rammed-earth walls were then given a plaster coat to prevent water erosion. Years later, the walls were given a coat of stucco to protect against dampness. Although the bell tower is massive, the church is well proportioned. The entranceway is through a round Norman arch — a style which is used throughout the church. The original square pews are still in use.

Among the early pioneers buried in the churchyard are Colonel O'Brien and his wife Mary, an imposing Celtic cross marking their grave. Their son, a renowned painter, is also buried there. (Lucius O'Brien's best-known painting, "Kakabeka Falls," hangs in the National Gallery of Canada in Ottawa.)

In the early days, many of the parishioners appeared in twos and threes from the surrounding woods, or paddled across the Bay in canoes, to come to the church in the clearing. To commemorate these early pioneers of Upper Canada who came so faithfully, an annual dockside service is still held each summer. But now, instead of the sound of paddles, the roar of motorboats pulling into the dock breaks the morning's silence. Situated in the rolling woodlands that reach down to the sparkling waters of Kempenfelt Bay, the clean lines of St. Thomas Anglican Church still create a delightful picture.

Peterborough County

15. Plymouth Brethren Chapel, 1839
Pengelly Landing, east of Bailieboro

What a friend we have in Jesus
All our sins and griefs to bear
What a privilege to carry
Every thing to God in prayer.

Joseph Scrivens (1820–1886)

In a small pioneer cemetery, near Bailieboro, not far from the northwest shore of Rice Lake, lies the mortal remains of one of Canada's most saintly preachers. Not many Canadians will recognize the name of Joseph Scrivens, but most Christian denominations are familiar with his universally famous hymn, "What a Friend we Have in Jesus."

Joseph Scrivens was born in County Down, Ireland, to Captain John and Jane Medlicott Scrivens. After attending Trinity College in Dublin, he was admitted to Addiscombe Military Seminary in 1837. Due to his strong aversion to military life and a supposedly delicate constitution, he returned to Trinity College, from which he graduated with a degree in theology.

Engaged to a lovely young lady, his future seemed secure but, on the very day of their wedding, tragedy struck. The young lovers had spent the afternoon horseback riding. Racing ahead, his bride-to-be jumped her horse over a fence and, landing in a water-filled ditch, was drowned. Traumatized by his fiancée's death, Scrivens at first immigrated to the Woodstock area in old Upper Canada. Then, during the 1850s, he moved from Woodstock to the district around Port Hope, where he was engaged by Captain R.L. Pengelly as a tutor.

The Pengelly family belonged to the Plymouth Brethren, an offshoot of the Anglican Church, whose teachings combined Pietism and Calvinism. Adhering to no organized ministry, they emphasized a literal translation of the Bible. Their Puritan morality appealed to the pious Scrivens and, joining the Brethren, he eventually became their most famous preacher.

In 1839 a small log chapel had been built on the Pengelly farm, as a place for pioneer families of the Plymouth Brethren faith to worship. A cemetery was laid out beside the chapel. It was here that Joseph Scrivens preached and worshipped until the building was demolished in 1879. Only drawings of the building survive; the adjacent cemetery is all that can be visited today.

While living with the Pengelly family, Scrivens met Mrs. Pengelly's niece, Catherine Roche. Once again, he fell in love. Before the couple were joined in wedlock, Catherine agreed to convert from the Church of England to the Plymouth Brethren faith. Part of the conversion involved baptism by total immersion. One day, in early April, the lovely Catherine was submerged in the icy waters of Rice Lake. Once again, tragedy struck: Catherine developed pneumonia and died before the wedding vows could be exchanged. She was buried in the Pengelly cemetery beside the log chapel. The grieving Scrivens erected a memorial stone to his beloved with the following inscription: "I shall be satisfied when I awake to see thy likeness."

Joseph Scrivens' grave.

Emulating the life of Christ, Joseph Scrivens devoted the rest of his days to the service of God. He preached on street corners in the nearby towns and villages of Northumberland and Peterborough Counties. Whenever he heard of a family in trouble, he was there to help. Every penny he earned went to the poor and needy.

One day, during winter, Scrivens met a poor shivering unfortunate on the street in Port Hope. Promptly, without questioning why the individual was in such a state, he removed his warm overcoat, sent to him from Ireland by his mother, and wrapped it around the man. Another time, when given the fare to attend a conference in Toronto, he walked all the way because he had given the money to a widow to feed her brood of hungry children.

It was while he lived on Strachan Street in Port Hope that Scrivens completed his famous hymn. He distributed copies over the years to friends in the area. Whenever anyone asked if he wrote the hymn, Scrivens would always reply, "The Lord and I did it between us."

An aura of mystery surrounds his death. A lifetime of devout service to God and self-deprivation had taken their toll on the elderly preacher. One wintry day a friend discovered he was missing; a search located his lifeless body in the nearby waters of Rice

A drawing of the Plymouth Brethen Chapel, Pengelly Landing, 1839–1879.

Lake. Was the very ill Scrivens drawn to the water in remembrance of his first sweetheart who had tumbled into the water-filled ditch, or was he called again to the baptism of his dearest Catherine?

On October 10, 1886, a rustic coffin containing the body of Joseph Scrivens was placed on a wagon. The cortège wound its way along the country road, ablaze with autumn colours, to come to its final resting place in Pengelly cemetery. In accordance with Scrivens' own wishes, he was interred near his beloved Catherine "in such position, with feet near feet, so that one day when we rise from the grave we will face one another."

Canada West
(1841–1866)

No part of Canada has ever been an entirely peaceable kingdom. In the midst of economic hard times, the Upper and Lower Canadian Rebellions of 1837–38 set the stage for the unusual short history of the so-called "United Province of Canada" (that is to say the southern parts of modern Ontario and Québec living restlessly together in a single house). Officially inaugurated by a simultaneous crash of cannon in Toronto and Montréal at twelve noon on February 10, 1841, it would be an era of many changes.

The old Upper Canada became the new Canada West section of the United Province. Over the next twenty-five years many of the characteristic modern institutions of both the subsequent Canadian confederation and the Canadian province of Ontario began to take shape.

Though the rebellions of the late 1830s were easily enough dealt with by the powers that be, they helped blaze a trail for Canadian self-rule within the British empire. By the end of the 1840s the elected legislators of the United Province had turned the old colonial regime of 1791 into "responsible government" — the beginnings of Canada's own version of what a later era would call constitutional monarchy and parliamentary democracy.

The new responsible legislature of the United Province gave the future Ontario the beginnings of its modern system of publicly funded popular education. With the legislature made up of equal numbers of representatives from both Canada West and Canada East (or modern Québec), there was some provision for publicly supported Separate Schools for Roman Catholics. But under the leadership of Egerton Ryerson (a Methodist minister who would serve as Canada West and then Ontario education superintendent from 1844 to 1876), a much larger and officially nonsectarian system of Public Schools was established, complete with a Normal School for training teachers.

The middle of the nineteenth century was a time of great innovations in transportation as well. In the 1850s the Grand Trunk Railway linked Montréal, Kingston, Toronto, Guelph, and Sarnia (on the border with Michigan). Other railroads were built connecting old Upper Canada to its former enemy, the United States. By 1858 the Great Western had linked Toronto, Hamilton, Niagara (on the border with New York State), London, and Windsor and Sarnia (on the border with Michigan again). The Northern Railway to Collingwood, on Georgian Bay, linked Toronto with the old Great Lakes water route to the Canadian Northwest.

Meanwhile, the Canada West that would become Ontario became the site of the first Canadian wheat boom. The first successful oil well in North America gushed forth at Oil Springs in the present-day southwestern part of the province. The first free trade agreement between Canada and the United States took effect between 1854 and 1866, and helped put the North American economy's assault on the Canadian forest into full bloom.

Fuelled especially by continuing immigration from various parts of Great Britain, the population of Canada West surged from some half million people in the early 1840s, to a million in the early 1850s, and a million and a half by the mid 1860s. Refugees from the potato famine in Ireland and the Highland Clearances in Scotland flocked into the backwoods of Canada West. With the gathering storm of the American Civil War on the horizon, Black Americans, escaping slavery on the Underground Railroad, found at least a safe and free haven of sorts on the Canadian side of the Detroit and Niagara Rivers.

Whatever their reasons for leaving their places of origin, the latest new arrivals were as attached to their churches as the pioneers of Upper Canada had been. The transformation of Bishop John Strachan's Anglican King's College into a more secularized University of Toronto, in 1849, was a sign that, in religion as in much else, the "mixed community" would dominate the future. People of various faiths were continuing to move to the region north of the Great Lakes. Some early dreams of the old colonial governing elite in Upper Canada had to be abandoned forever. Amidst the many changes of the mid-nineteenth century in Canada West, it was at last officially decided that there would be no official or established religion, even in a province that remained so loyal to the United Empire.

Grenville County

16. The Blue Church (Anglican), 1845
Highway 2, west of Prescott

And so were the churches established in the
faith, and increased in numbers daily.
Acts 16:5

The case for the Church of England as the official religion of Upper Canada might have been somewhat stronger if the great majority of the original Loyalists of the 1780s and 1790s had been Anglicans. But this was not the case. One United Empire Loyalist who would leave an indelible mark on the future province of Ontario was the Methodist pioneer, Barbara Heck.

Barbara was born in Ireland in 1734, to parents from a unique community of "Palatine Methodists." (These were Protestant refugees from religious persecution in the Palatinate, in the southern part of present-day Germany, who had become early converts to the preaching of John Wesley after they fled to Ireland.) Along with her husband, Paul, and others from the community, Barbara Heck moved to colonial America in 1760.

One day, several years later, the feisty Barbara came upon some friends playing cards. Fearful that the devil had invaded their home, Barbara snatched the cards and flung them into the fireplace. Not satisfied that her friends had been chastened, the devout lady persuaded her cousin, Philip Embury, to become their religious leader. From that episode, some say, the first Methodist church in North America was founded in 1766.

When the American Revolution broke out, Barbara Heck and her husband Paul joined a group of United Empire Loyalists who moved to Montréal, and then made their way to the Augusta area in present-day eastern Ontario. If William Losee is considered the father of Methodism in Upper Canada, then Barbara Heck must be considered its mother. She was already on hand to greet him when he arrived in 1790.

Some of the Loyalists of Upper Canada, of course, certainly were adherents of the Church of England — which was the established religion of the mother country.

*Barbara Heck's monument in the cemetery of
The Blue Church, near Prescott.*

Sometime in the early 1800s, an especially memorable group of Barbara Heck's Anglican neighbours in Augusta Township, Grenville County, held a meeting to plan the building of a church. They had no sooner finished the building when it went up in flames.

Not daunted by the loss, the Anglican community in Augusta built another church. During the early days of Canada West, in the 1840s, fire struck again and the church was destroyed once more. In 1845, it was rebuilt yet another and final time. (There would be a third fire in 1903, but the damage was not extensive and the church was repaired.) As was the original, the church as it stands today is painted blue — the traditional colour of loyalty, which in eastern Ontario became a particular symbol of the at least largely Protestant body of United Empire Loyalists.

Back in the pioneering Upper Canada of 1804, while sitting in her chair reading her large German Bible, Barbara Heck had quietly slipped into her last sleep. Although a fervent Methodist, she was interred in what is now the Anglican Blue Church cemetery. A hundred years after her death a large stone monument in her honour was paid for by public subscription and placed in the cemetery.

Still an appealing, well-tended structure, the Blue Church today attracts hundreds of tourists annually. United Church folk, Anglicans, and those of many other denominations come to pay homage to Barbara Heck. Other tourists click their cameras for a picture of one of the most photographed old church buildings in Canada.

Kent County
(Municipality of Chatham-Kent)

17. New Fairfield Church, 1848
Moraviantown, east of Thamesville

> *Fairfield is a garden of the Lord in which he has*
> *planted many trees which were originally wild.*
> Fairfield Church Diary, July 28, 1798

*A*nother memorable present-day church building which dates back to Canada West in the 1840s has deeper roots in the earlier pioneer days of Upper Canada.

The Battle of the Thames had been an important event in the War of 1812–14. Here, near the village of Moraviantown, the Delaware Chief Tecumseh led eight hundred warriors to the aid of the British Crown. Unable to stop a fierce American charge, the warriors lost heart when their leader fell mortally wounded on the battlefield. Today a small park dedicated to Tecumseh's memory has been laid out on the ground where he was killed. No stone marks his grave: only a grassy sward carpets the place where he and his followers fought and died.

From this small park, through the buckthorns and wild berry bushes, one can just glimpse a small, white clapboard church. This points to the main part of the story. In May 1792, an unusual group of settlers had arrived from the new American republic to take up land above the Thames River in present-day southwestern Ontario. Led by a Moravian missionary, David Zeisberger, a band of Delaware had made a cold and perilous crossing of Lake St. Clair. They had come to find a new home where they hoped to be free from the persecution that had plagued them in the land where they began. Originally from the shadowy, fragrant forests and valleys along the Delaware River, in what is now New Jersey, Delaware, and eastern Pennsylvania, these particular first peoples had been converted to Christianity by Moravian missionaries.

These missionaries, whose homeland was in the present-day Czech Republic, belonged to the oldest Protestant church in existence. In 1457, sixty years before Luther's Reformation, the Moravian movement had been founded by followers of John Huss, the Bohemian martyr who later burned at the stake for his beliefs. The Moravians subsequently came to the New World with one purpose: to love the first peoples as

New Fairfield Church, Moraviantown.

brothers and to bring to them the Gospel of Christ. Coming from strife-torn Europe, the gentle customs of this pious brotherhood made an uncommon religion. Unitas Fratrum (or United Brethren), the formal name of the Moravians, reflects their motto: "In essentials, unity; in nonessentials, liberty; in all things, love."

Unfortunately, the Moravian missionaries did not find the peace and freedom that they had hoped for in America. In 1782 ninety of their Delaware converts — men, women and children from one village — had been slaughtered by forces on the side of the American Revolution. After a decade of continuing persecution by the new frontier settlers who rushed westward when the revolution triumphed, the Delaware and their missionaries accepted an offer of asylum in Canada. Led by the seventy-year-old David Zeisberger, they settled on the banks of the Thames. A new Upper Canadian community, dedicated as Hutberg and later renamed New Fairfield, took shape. A temporary church was erected in four days, and the first service was held in May 1792.

The rest of the community soon took shape. The Moravian Delaware lived in houses made of logs, with split cedar shingles and central fireplaces, and they farmed the land. Their settlement had more than forty houses, an assortment of farm outbuildings, two schools, and a church. For a time they enjoyed peace and prosperity in what they described as "a garden of the Lord."

Their Easter celebrations, which involved daily services during Passion Week, had fascinating features. Each evening, readings of the Lord's Passion and Resurrection were interspersed with antiphonal chorales and hymns, accompanied by trombones. The customary washing of feet, with men and women separated, took place on Wednesday. On Friday, the story of the Crucifixion was reviewed and an impressive liturgy was read. Saturday was the Quiet Sabbath, followed by a love feast — a simple meal of bread and tea or coffee, enjoyed after Communion.

The greatest event was saved for Easter Sunday: a traditional symbolic sunrise service. Before the first bird call, the sound of the bell summoned the faithful to the chapel, where the congregation greeted each other with the orthodox salutation, "The Lord is Risen." Then they walked along the still, shadowy path to some graves in a field nearby and, in the Unami tongue (a Delaware dialect), David Zeisberger said the Easter Morning Litany, embodying the Moravian Confession of Faith. As the sun's brightening rays lit up the morning sky, a hymn of resurrection, faith, and hope poured forth from the throats of the Delaware faithful. As the warmth of the sun warmed their heads, the service ended with the conventional benediction.

The congregation's original log church had double doorways, cut through on the sides of the building. Light streamed through a pair of shuttered windows between the canopied doorways. This little building was eventually considered inadequate and was replaced by the present clapboard church in 1848 — more than a generation after the Battle of the Thames (and also the year that "responsible government" finally arrived in Canada West).

The Fairfield settlement was the only enterprise of its sort undertaken by Moravian missionaries in Canada. Even here, the continuing growth of Canada West and its successor province of Ontario would soon enough overshadow their work. In 1902 the Moravian missionaries transferred their property in southwestern Ontario to the Canadian Methodist Episcopal Church. By this time new troubles had turned the old Moravian Delaware community into a shadow of its former self. In 1925 responsibility for the maintenance and repair of the church building of 1848 fell into the hands of the new United Church of Canada. Today the modest white clapboard church at New Fairfield still stands as solitary witness to the work of the devoted Moravian missionaries among the Delaware — and to the Canadian sacrifices of Tecumseh and his fallen warriors, whose final resting place can still be glimpsed from the grounds of the building.

Lanark County

18. St. John the Baptist Roman Catholic Church, 1848
38 Wilson Street East, Perth

He that smiteth a man, so that he die,
shall be surely put to death.
Exodus 21:12

Scotland was a major source of immigrants to Canada throughout the nineteenth century, and large numbers of Scots settled in Lanark County, in present-day eastern Ontario. But there were also important concentrations of Irish in the area. Often living in desperate straits in their then-impoverished homeland, they came in search of land and a better way of life. In the great age of sailing ships, Irish, like other immigrants on a budget, frequently lived through quite stormy crossings of the Atlantic Ocean which lasted ten to twelve weeks. The unfortunate passengers were subjected to cramped quarters with foul air, lack of exercise, and bad food.

Although not the first church in the town of Perth (the county seat of Lanark), St. John the Baptist Roman Catholic Church, built on four acres of land in the Canada West banner year of 1848, is the oldest surviving church structure in the place today. Commanding a view of the surrounding vicinity, the church, manse, and school are situated on the highest elevation in the community — a location characteristic of Irish Catholic churches in nineteenth-century Ontario. St. John the Baptist in Perth also shows the influence of the Dublin architect, John Semple, who created what is termed spiked Gothic in Irish church architecture. The name "St. John" honours the memory of an Irish priest, Father John H. McDonough.

Perth, Ontario, itself, named after Perth in Scotland, is one of the most historically interesting towns in the province today. Its beginnings go back to some four thousand Scottish and Irish settlers who came to Lanark County via Brockville between 1816 and 1822. One thousand of the group were former British military personnel. The adjacent Tay River was eventually converted into a canal, which connects Perth to Lower Rideau Lake and the Rideau Canal. A series of locks allows small vessels to navigate the waterway. In the dynamic days of Canada West, a tow path allowed heavily laden barges to be poled up the canal from Lower Rideau Lake.

On any walking tour through the quiet streets of the present-day town, one must visit the Matheson House. Built in 1840 by the area's wealthiest citizen, it is now the Perth museum. It is home to what is said to be the oldest physical evidence of life on this planet, a climaclichnite or giant snail that lived five hundred million years ago. A snippet of a prize-winning 2000-pound cheese manufactured in Perth is preserved in the museum as well. Outside is an 1840s garden, home to many varieties of roses grown by the early settlers. It makes an especially pleasant break to visit the round Garden for the Blind. This peaceful retreat off Sunset Boulevard has large, waist-high planters with flora especially chosen for their texture and smell.

Further along on the walking tour, one should pause in front of

St. John the Baptist Roman Catholic Church, Perth.

the court house, built circa 1842, on the corner of Craig and Drummond Streets. On a Saturday morning in May 1851, the last public execution in Perth took place in front of this building. Francis Beare suffered the full measure of the law for the murder of William Barry. A large group of citizens, including a number of respectfully dressed women, gathered to witness the unpleasant spectacle. Without a pause, the culprit, clothed in white raiment and cap, ascended the gallows platform. Earlier that morning,

Father John H. McDonough had administered the last rites to the prisoner. Two other priests accompanied the condemned man on the gallows platform. The unhappy wretch had confessed to committing the murder by striking two blows to the unfortunate victim, claiming his wife had urged him to do it. In supplication, the condemned man knelt on the platform and, in a firm voice, repeated the prayers of the Church. Silently, glancing at the crowd, he took his place under the gallows and met his fate.

It is claimed that the sheriff had difficulty securing a hangman. As a last resort, he was able to obtain the assistance of a prisoner in Kingston Penitentiary by promising a pardon. The prisoner was escorted to Perth by guards and kept in the jail overnight. The community, incensed at the idea of a prisoner hangman, threatened to lynch the executioner. After the execution, the authorities had to conceal him in a vault in the Registry Office. From there he was secretly taken below the Red Bridge, where he awaited the stage coach to take him via Smiths Falls to Brockville and thence to Kingston. Whether he received a pardon is not recorded.

St. John the Baptist Church in Perth, built of local limestone, is considered to be of incomparable design for its Canada West time and place. The severely plain walls are broken by tall lancet windows. Supporting a graceful spire, an unusually narrow tower is flanked by corner turrets almost as large as the tower. The vaulted interior is reached through three Gothic portals. Composite piers separate the spacious nave from the side aisles. A hundred years after its construction, a student of the subject described the building as "one of the noblest remaining from the midcentury. Few church designs of the period can compare with it."

Continuing to stroll through the town, with its market air, one feels that history is very much alive. Above the modern shopfronts, the eye catches the line of grey stone buildings, reminiscent of a world that has now almost entirely vanished in other parts of Ontario today.

19. St. James the Apostle Anglican Church, 1861
Drummond Street, Perth

20. St. Andrew's Presbyterian Church, 1928
Drummond Street, Perth

The churches of Perth are a mighty power for good.
There is no unseemly strife among them ...
The brethren dwell in unity.
Perth Expositor, May 14, 1896

*H*ad the late nineteenth-century author of this celebration of harmony among the churches of Perth looked back in time, he might have changed his mind. On June 13, 1833, the town was the site of the last fatal duel in Upper Canada. One of the parties to the conflict was an Anglican, and the other a Presbyterian.

After the War of 1812–14, the religious aspect of the conflict went back to the founding of Perth. Fearful that the single line of communication along the St. Lawrence River between Montréal and the western part of Upper Canada could easily be broken by American forces in some future struggle, British military officials decided that a secondary route along the Ottawa and Rideau Rivers was necessary, and this led to the construction of the Rideau Canal. For the protection of the route, loyal British army veterans of long service were encouraged to settle in the wilderness beyond the Rideau. They were attracted by free passage across the ocean, land grants, and, for each family, a free hammer, saw, chisel, nails, grindstone, auger, pot, kettle, and blankets. In exchange, they would provide a trained militia in the event of future hostilities.

Because many of the original immigrants attracted to the area under these terms were from Scotland, the Auld Kirk from across the ocean quickly established itself in the new settlement around Perth. The first church built in the town, in 1819, was Presbyterian — a wood frame structure with a spire and bell, seating a congregation of four hundred. Just as Canada West was turning into the modern province of Ontario, in 1867, this building was destroyed by fire. However, the original bell was saved, and it still hangs in the present St. Andrew's Presbyterian Church building in Perth, which dates back to as recently as 1928.

Regardless of its eventual fate north of the Great Lakes, the Church of England

St Andrew's Presbyterian Church, Perth.

would also remain the official religion of the British army. Religious services for the military were always held according to Church of England rites. Thus Anglicans established themselves early on as an important force in Perth as well. Not to be outdone by the Presbyterians, they built St. James, the first Anglican church in the town, in 1820. In 1836, the Lieutenant Governor of Upper Canada, Sir John A. Colborne, on behalf of King William IV, presented a Royal Charter to St. James Anglican Church in Perth. (This allowed the wearing of scarlet cassocks and other royal accouterments in the church.) The present church building replaced the original wood frame structure in 1861, and still dates back to the later days of Canada West.

The military character of the new settlement at Perth similarly provided a climate for affairs of honour, which were frequent occurrences but generally ended harmlessly. The last fatal duel in Upper Canada, fought at Perth on June 13, 1833, was different. Although the participants in this tragic event were a Presbyterian and an Anglican, the subject of the dispute was Elizabeth Hughes, the daughter of a Unitarian minister. The protagonist, the twenty-four-year-old Presbyterian, John Wilson, was a law student and the son of a poor but respectable weaver from Scotland. John fell in love with Elizabeth, and began to court her by inscribing his emotions in verse. His antagonist in the duel, nineteen-year-old Robert Lyon, Church of England, was also a law student, but from a family of greater local consequence. His brother, an ex-officer who had been wounded at the Battle of Chippawa, was among of the British military personnel who settled in the area. Robert came to Upper Canada to live with his brother.

There is some confusion as to the exact cause of the duel. It seems that some of Wilson's poetic endeavors fell into the wrong hands and were used by Lyon's friends to trigger the event. Wilson, feeling rejected, commented disparagingly on the nature of Miss Hughes. Lyon, who was described as a crack shot, took it upon himself to defend the lady's honour. An attempt was made by friends to bring the disputing parties to an amicable settlement. Before the actual duel took place, the two men had a meeting during which Lyon struck Wilson and bloodied his face. The reluctant Wilson tried to settle the matter by asking for an apology from Lyon. The rather hotheaded Lyon was eager for a showdown and refused. Wilson, conscious of his lowly origins and concerned that he would not be respected in the community, issued the challenge. In accordance with established protocol, seconds were chosen, and a time and place agreed upon. On a rainy, mosquito-infested evening, the contestants trudged along a road to a grassy field near the Tay River to defend their honour.

At first, although it sounded like a lone gunshot, both parties had discharged their weapons simultaneously and remained unscathed. A reconciliation would probably have taken place had not Lyon's second insisted that the combatants try again. Then Wilson, seeing Lyon pointing his weapon at him, turned his head aside and raising his gun, fired the fatal shot. Mortally wounded, Lyon fell on the wet grass.

Wilson and his second surrendered

St James the Apostle Anglican Church, Perth.

immediately to the authorities and were lodged in jail. The jury, consisting mostly of men who considered duelling an honourable activity, took only a short time to return a not-guilty verdict. Wilson's trial was not over, however: he still had to face his peers in the Presbyterian church. After being admonished and serving a three-month suspension from Communion, he was reinstated and ultimately served as treasurer and trustee at St. Andrew's. Soon he also passed his bar examinations, and eventually he became a judge. Ironically, the first court over which he presided was in Brockville, where he himself had stood trial. Legend has it that, during his time on the bench, he would never pronounce a death sentence. Three years after the duel, John Wilson and Elizabeth Hughes were joined in holy wedlock. Later in life, Wilson became a Member of Parliament for London, Ontario.

The less fortunate Robert Lyon was carried to the veranda of his uncle's house in Perth. On the following Saturday, from the pulpit of St. James Church, the Reverend Michael Harris read the funeral service for Robert Lyon. Over his grave in the Anglican section of the old burying ground in Perth is a small, weatherworn headstone. The journal of the Reverend William Bell, the first Presbyterian minister in the area, records that, only a month before the duel, Robert Lyon had been visited by a premonition of his death. He dreamed that he had walked past the burying grounds wearing his grave clothes.

One of the main exhibits in the Matheson House museum in Perth today is the brace of pistols used in the last fatal duel in Upper Canada. In memory of the infamous event, a local campground on the Tay River is named Last Duel Campground. Visitors continue to be welcomed as well at St. James and St. Andrew's, and any of the Perth churches. Like many other historic buildings in the town, the churches are part of a still thriving community which takes pride in a fascinating local heritage.

Middlesex County

21. St. Patrick's Roman Catholic Church, 1858
Lucan, north of London

*Thou shalt not covet thy neighbour's house ... nor
any thing that is thy neighbour's.*
Exodus 20:17

The village of Lucan, in the London area of present-day southwestern Ontario (where John Wilson from Perth finally became a Member of Parliament), has its own fascinating heritage. This starts with St. Patrick's Roman Catholic Church, visible from a distance and set apart from the village itself. With its dominating spire atop a square brick tower, St. Patrick's is similar in style to other Catholic buildings that date back to the age of Canada West.

The church is named after the well-known patron saint of Ireland. By the later nineteenth century "Irish" would be the single largest Old World ethnic origin in Ontario, but this included both Protestants (and the infamous Orangemen) and Roman Catholics. Unfortunately, religious and other feuds from the old country were often transported intact.

The village of Lucan and the surrounding farmland of Biddulph Township attracted many Irish settlers. Until 1850, when a log church was built on five acres of land donated by James Kelly, the Catholic population was ministered to by missionary priests from nearby London and St. Thomas. In 1854, Father Peter Francis Crinnon became St. Patrick's first resident priest. The log church was replaced in 1858 by the brick building still in use today.

The best-known part of the parish's history starts back in the early 1840s, when James and Johannah Donnelly immigrated to Canada West from County Tipperary, Ireland. After living briefly in London, they moved north to Biddulph Township, with their two young sons, and took up residence on Lot 18, on the sixth concession of the Roman Line. Too poor to buy land legally, James had decided to squat on some unoccupied land. Squatting was a relatively common way for the poor to acquire land in those

The modern Donnelly family gravestone in the cemetery of St. Patrick's Church, Lucan.

days and many years often passed before a squatter's claim was challenged. The Donnellys began to clear the land and to establish a farm. Their family eventually grew to include seven sons and one daughter.

Most of the township's early population were also from Tipperary, and they did bring many of the feuds and superstitions of the old country with them. Fist fights were not uncommon. Arson and the mutilation of livestock increased as the feuding escalated. James Donnelly in particular angered some of the local residents by donating money to help build an Anglican church in the township. James's second son, nicknamed "Clubfoot Will," had been born with a deformed foot, which some believed to be the mark of Satan. The Donnellys were involved in the feuding that plagued Biddulph Township, but not more, it would seem, than many other families.

In 1855, John Grace, the absent owner of the land upon which the Donnellys lived, sold part of his property to Michael Maher, who then rented it to one Patrick Farrell. James Donnelly refused to vacate and he and Farrell ended up arguing the matter in court. James was allowed to keep the northern fifty acres but was forced to give up the southern half of the land. The resulting feud between the two men culminated in a fight at a logging bee on June 25, 1857, in which Farrell was killed.

James Donnelly, now a murderer, disappeared for eleven months. After hiding on his own land through the long winter, he turned himself in the following May. He stood trial in Goderich, Canada West, was convicted, and sentenced to hang on September 17, 1858. His wife, Johannah, petitioned the court for clemency, however, and the sentence was lightened. After serving seven years in Kingston Penitentiary, James returned to Biddulph Township in 1865.

Meanwhile, James's seven sons had acquired quite a reputation among their neighbours. They were a tough bunch, always ready to fight and in constant trouble with the law. Their father's incarceration had intensified the taunts directed towards the family and they had become local scapegoats. Every crime that took place in the area was blamed on them, regardless of whether they were the real perpetrators. Over the next fifteen years, the Donnellys continued to act as a lightning rod for continued feuding in Biddulph Township.

Early in February 1880 the tension would explode. By this time only the youngest son, Thomas, remained at home. Two of the Donnelly boys, James Jr. and Michael, had already died, and daughter Jane, the youngest of the family, had moved to St. Thomas after her marriage. The remaining four boys had married and moved out of their parents' home. Bridget Donnelly, a cousin visiting from Ireland, was staying with the family, as was eleven-year-old Johnny O'Connor, a neighbour boy who had been brought over to look after the pigs. The four Donnellys and Johnny O'Connor retired on the night of February 3, unaware that a vigilante committee planned to descend upon the house.

In the early hours of February 4, the family was awakened by someone pounding on the door. James Donnelly, who was sharing his bed with young Johnny O'Connor, got up to see what was going on. A group of perhaps twenty men, some dressed in women's clothing, and armed with clubs, sticks, and other farm implements, proceeded to cruelly beat the four Donnellys to death before setting the house on fire. Johnny O'Connor, who hid under the bed at the first sign of trouble, survived and would later be a witness at the trial of the accused.

The gang continued down the road to the home of William Donnelly. Clubfoot Will was considered the smartest of the family and the vigilantes were keen to get rid of him. They pounded on his door shouting, "Fire!" John Donnelly was spending the night at his brother's house and it was he who opened the door to receive the dozens of gunshots meant for William. Oblivious to the mistake, the gang left, satisfied they had eliminated Clubfoot Will.

Six of the murderers were identified by Johnny O'Connor and William Donnelly and brought to trial in London. The first trial, in September of 1880, resulted in a hung jury; the second jury returned a verdict of "not guilty" in January 1881.

The day of the multiple funeral, St. Patrick's Roman Catholic Church was packed, hundreds being unable to get in. As the mass for the repose of souls was sung, those assembled gave vent to their pent-up feelings and broke into tears.

The two coffins — one containing the body of John Donnelly, the other the charred, combined remains of James, Johannah, Thomas, and Bridget Donnelly — were interred in the cemetery of St. Patrick's. The famous tombstone with "murdered" under each name was erected by William Donnelly in 1889. Over the years, vandals and tourists caused enough damage to the stone and to the church grounds that the marker was removed in 1964. It is only in recent years that a new stone has been installed to mark the grave. The simple inscription reads: "May their souls rest in peace." One hopes that they will, at last.

Glengarry County

22. Gordon Presbyterian Church, 1864
St. Elmo, north of Maxville

*Not wealth, not enterprise, not energy can build
a nation into greatness, but man, and only men
with the fear of God in their hearts... .*
Charles William Gordon (1860–1937)

*M*any children born in the rising Canada West would have careers that stretched well into the twentieth century. A special example is Charles William Gordon, who was born in Glengarry County in eastern Ontario in 1860, and who would leave a lasting mark on the development of the Protestant church in Canada.

Charles Gordon (also known as Ralph Connor), was the son of a Presbyterian minister who came to Canada West from the Scottish Highlands in the 1840s. Charles was educated at the Universities of Toronto and Edinburgh. Ordained in 1890, he began his outstanding career as a missionary in the Banff area of present-day Alberta — which was then a part of the Northwest Territories where the Canadian fur trade had only begun to give way to the family farm. During the First World War, Major Gordon served as a chaplain in France. In 1921 he became the moderator of the Presbyterian Church of Canada and, in 1925, he helped form the United Church of Canada.

Although he used literature to preach his particular brand of energetic Christianity, Charles Gordon is remembered more today for his detailed descriptions of the lives of Canadian pioneers with ancestral roots in the Western Isles and glens of Scotland. He became one of the new country's leading authors in the early twentieth century, under the pen name Ralph Connor. His books drew on his boyhood memories of Glengarry County and his experiences in the Canadian West. He wrote what is considered his finest novel, *The Man from Glengarry*, in 1901. It is both the story of a land "shaped into a nation by work, prayer, and love," and one of the first works of fiction to capture the real human characters who lived in such places as Glengarry County, Ontario, in the nineteenth century.

Many Scottish immigrants to Canada had been driven from their native land by the

Gordon Presbyterian Church, St. Elmo.

harsh clan chieftains who wanted more room for sheep pastures. They carried in their blood the fierce passions, courage, and loyalty that marked them as Highlanders. But the biggest thing in them was the faith that coursed through their veins to their very hearts' core. The strict and somber religion that put the fear of God into men's souls, and the love of God into men's hearts, was the foundation upon which they would help create the Canada we know today.

With great warmth and understanding, Charles Gordon (or Ralph Connor, if you prefer) described the humbler aspects of the early days of the Scottish settlements. Many scenes are taken from real life. His pages are filled with stories of the struggle for survival on the harsh Canadian Shield of eastern Ontario. Ontario school readers used to include his dramatic story of young Ranald, pursued by a band of ravening wolves, riding for his life through the dense forests of Glengarry County. On a dark winter evening, many rural children of the 1930s, expecting at any moment to see a long grey shadow slink out of the bush, peered anxiously over their shoulders as they trudged along a snowy dirt road on their way home from school.

Gordon's novel, *Glengarry School Days*, portrays the influence of church and school on the lives of the Scottish settlers. The book captures a way of life that has disappeared from the Canadian scene. The old one-room log schoolhouse and the masters who left an indelible imprint on the minds, souls, and backsides of the youth of the rural community are but memories now. (The log schoolhouse which Gordon himself attended, the model on which he based *Glengarry School Days*, has been moved to the present-day Upper Canada Village near Morrisburg).

Gordon also gives his readers a historical account of the first church in which his father preached, in the Glengarry County hamlet of St. Elmo. Constructed on the edge of the forest near the manse, it was built in the no-nonsense fashion of early Presbyterian doctrine. The weather-beaten, black-knotted clapboard exterior, resembling a barn, sported neither steeple nor tower to soften its harsh outline. A peek through the uncurtained windows into the yellowing pine interior revealed a gallery along three sides. The main body of the church contained box pews whose hinged doors were marked with the names of paid-up members.

The octagonal pulpit, reached by a high staircase, perched high on one side, level with the gallery. From this vantage point, the preacher kept an eagle eye on his flock. Any miscreant who dared to be distracted by the stealthy creak of the opening door would soon straighten around as the minister thundered forth in Gaelic: "Give you heed to me and I will let you know who the latecomers are." No sinner in the congregation could hide from the wrathful eye of God above, or the more immediate gaze of the preacher in the pulpit below. The canopy and the highly ornate sounding board (forerunner of the modern loudspeaker system) hung over the pulpit. The elders' square pew occupied the area directly below. The precentor, leader of the psalmody, sat at a desk that was part of the pulpit. The old Scottish custom of "lining" the psalms survived from the time when psalm books were scarce, and the precentor alone chanted each line.

In 1864, when Charles Gordon himself was still a very young boy, the present red brick church replaced the original structure, which, having outgrown its usefulness, was torn down. The new church, with its simple interior, contrasted sharply with the drafty old clapboard building. A stained glass window fitted in the wall over the entrance gave colourful relief to the plastered walls. The arched windows along both sides allowed amber light to stream across the worshippers' heads as they bowed in prayer.

The preacher no longer kept track of his congregation from a high crow's nest: he addressed them from a modest pulpit on a raised platform. The precentor's desk was absent, and the elders sat with their families in new curved oak pews. The opening services in the new church were held on the first Thursday of the Communion season. To the orthodox, self-reliant Highland Presbyterians, this was the great occasion of the year. Associated with the Lord's Supper, it was strictly observed. No meals were cooked until after the services and, as these sometimes went on all day, there were many hungry people by nightfall.

Today the well-cared-for Gordon Presbyterian Church at St. Elmo, where the young Charles Gordon was indoctrinated into the Christian faith, stands on a slight rise, a simple cross on the plain steeple starkly outlined against the bright blue of a clear summer sky. The interior of the church has been kept as it was in the early days. The cast-iron box stove, whose pipes run the full length of the room, is still used for heating. One can sit in the very back pew once reserved for the minister's family and, closing one's eyes, imagine listening to a thunderous sermon of fire and brimstone that reached into every corner of the church. Gone are the encircling forests of an earlier era, and the howl of wolves are merely echoes in some old-timer's dream. The hum of traffic and the roar of a farmer's tractor are the only sounds that shatter the silence of a summer's day. But a visitor to the church of The Man from Glengarry can still detect a trace of the soft Gaelic lilt in the speech of the local people — perhaps the last remnant of the old Highland roots.

23. Congregational Church, 1837
St. Elmo, north of Maxville

Thou shalt love thy neighbour as thyself.
Mark 12:31

The present-day Glengarry County hamlet of St. Elmo is also home to a structure that actually dates back to the year of the Upper Canadian Rebellion, which set the stage for the creation of Canada West. Just a short stroll across the road from Gordon Presbyterian Church is an old log building, erected in 1837. It is one of the oldest remaining Congregational churches to be built in what is now Ontario, and one of the now rather small number of old log churches of any denomination that still survive.

Generally, it has been said, Congregationalism is what the Protestant Reformation or Puritan movement first created in England, just as it created Presbyterianism in Scotland. The English Puritans who landed at Plymouth Rock in 1620 and went on to establish the New England colonies were Congregationalists, and they also established the Congregational church in America. In between the cracks of real life, however, there were some English Presbyterians and some Scottish Congregationalists. Some of them eventually wound up in the New World as well.

Congregational Church, St. Elmo.

In particular, the members of the Congregational "Little Kirk" in St. Elmo, who built their very simple log house of worship in 1837, were as Scottish as their Presbyterian brethren. The Little Kirk was nonetheless a poor cousin to Gordon Presbyterian Church, especially after the construction of the present red brick Presbyterian building with its grand steeple and arched windows.

At first the Presbyterians of St. Elmo were on quite friendly terms with their Congregationalist brethren. Charles Gordon's mother, the wife of the Presbyterian minister, had grown up in the Congregationalist faith. But the generation born during the rising age of Canada West had feelings of rivalry towards their neighbours that bordered on animosity. To the younger Presbyterians, even the name Little Kirk had a contemptible ring.

One day, while passing the place, Charles Gordon and his brother paused. The small, unprotected glass windows of the simple log building glowed in the sunlight. Charles and his brother apparently saw this as an affront to their grander church just across the way. Denominational zeal seized Charles and he snatched a stone which somehow flew from his hand and through a pane of glass. His brother, fired up by the tinkling sound, found a larger rock. Soon it was a contest to see who could throw best.

Pioneering Spirit

When all the windows had been broken, the enormity of the Gordon brothers' transgression dawned on them. Filled with a sense of doom, and fearing a trip to the woodshed, they made themselves scarce. Although the Congregationalists were very aware of the miscreants' identity, no complaint reached the ears of the boys' parents. Because of the high esteem and affection the Gordon family enjoyed in the community, a forgiving congregation quietly replaced the windows.

On another occasion Charles Gordon's father called a meeting to denounce a young Baptist student, who was said to be trying to seduce a local maiden. Reverend Gordon characterized the young man as an irredeemable reprobate. Reverend MacDougall, the first minister of the Congregational Church, chided his volatile Presbyterian colleague, and defended the young man, saying, "I am distressed to have to interrupt you in the House of God. But much as I disapprove of the young man, surely you know that what you are saying about him is not true." The contrite Reverend Gordon burst into tears and replied, "You are quite right. Let us pray."

In 1870 the Reverend William Peacock would become the second minister appointed to the Congregational Church in St. Elmo. A man of strong convictions, he would not allow a meeting promoting the temperance movement to be held in the church: any discussion on such a hell-born topic was bound to defile the building.

The Reverend Peacock's son, ultimately known as Sir Edward Peacock, was one of various interesting and unusually successful people who came out of small communities in rural Ontario during the nineteenth century. Edward Peacock was born in the humble manse of the Congregational log church in St. Elmo. Educated at Queen's University in Kingston, he eventually became financial advisor to four British monarchs: George V, Edward VIII, George VI, and Elizabeth II. For his assistance to the Crown, George V awarded him the monarch's personal knighthood, the Grand Cross of the Victorian Order. As the receiver general for the Duchy of Cornwall, Sir Edward played a role in the abdication of Edward VIII. During the Second World War, he had the difficult task of managing British securities in the United States, to help Winston Churchill purchase munitions. His astute work on behalf of the Rhodes trust ensured that endowment funds would be in place for future Rhodes scholars.

Sir Edward once recalled that his uncle, William MacAllister, another Congregational preacher, was of the strictest Puritan ethics. The sermons of the day were very long and filled with threats of hellfire. On a hot and steamy Sunday, the reverend's daughter, Isabella, a young lady of twenty, dozed off. A stern voice, carrying to every corner of the room, ordered: "Isabella MacAllister, leave this house at once and get you home to bed." History does not record whether the embarrassed Isabella went to bed, but she promptly got up and left the service.

The stern preacher was not entirely without a sense of humour. One Sunday, one of his rather pompous male parishioners fell asleep. The man's head sagged on the pew and his full wig slid to the floor. Unfortunately, a local shepherd happened to be present with his dog. (Scottish custom allowed shepherds on duty to come to church with their dog in tow). Mistaking the fallen hairpiece for a rabbit, the dog grabbed it and with accompanying growls began to shake the devil out of it. To conceal his laughter, the preacher slid to the floor behind the pulpit.

Remarkably enough, the well-preserved Congregational Church of 1837 in St. Elmo, Glengarry County is still intact, though its logs are sagging today. Last occupied for strictly religious purposes in 1912, it is now used as a hall for the local Women's Institute.

District of Cochrane

24. St. Thomas Anglican Church, 1864
Front Road, Moose Factory

*The happiest man is he who is most diligently
employed about His Master's business.*
John Horden (1828–1893)

Officially, the geography of the Canada West section of the United Province, like Upper Canada, was largely confined to present-day southern Ontario. In the early 1860s almost all of what is now northern Ontario was still part of the vast Canadian fur-trading wilderness loosely managed by the Hudson's Bay Company (which had merged with its chief rival, the North West Company, as long ago as 1821).

Henry Hudson, however, had arrived in the vast northern body of water that now bears his name in 1610. In 1673 the new Hudson's Bay Company had established the first permanent English-speaking settlement in present-day Ontario, on what is now called Moose Factory Island (or just Moose Factory), in the middle of the Moose River, a short distance in from James Bay.

While no magnet for settlers in the style of down south, the life of the old "Indian and European" fur trade way up north was still attracting some new arrivals from across the ocean in the age of Canada West. To help bring the comforts of the Church of England to what was still a very rugged existence, in June 1851 the young missionary John Horden and his wife set sail from Gravesend, England, bound for the already quite old Hudson's Bay Company trading post at Moose Factory. As it entered Hudson Bay from Hudson Strait, the ship was armed with thick blocks of timber at the bow, known as ice chocks, to do battle with the ice floes it encountered. After a perilous trip through floating ice that constantly battered the ship, passengers and crew were greeted with cries of "chimo" (welcome in Inuit) and passed through the Strait into the Bay. But the danger was not over. The ship was subsequently imprisoned in ice for three weeks, and there was concern that its sides would be crushed. Suddenly, with a roar like thunder, the ice cracked and a passage opened. The weary passengers and crew gave thanks as they finally landed on the island in the mouth of the Moose River, in the southwest corner of James Bay.

For the next forty-two years, John Horden ministered to the handfuls of Hudson's Bay Company employees and the much more numerous Cree and Inuit in what is now the far north of Ontario. A scholar of languages, he learned both Cree and Inuit, and he eventually translated the Bible into Cree so that "my people will have the word of God in a form they can understand." He also taught himself Hebrew, to read the Bible in the first language of the Old Testament. His Sunday services began at 6:00 a.m. and continued throughout the day and into the evening. When he wasn't preaching, he was teaching, and he often served as a rudimentary medical doctor.

Horden was ordained as both deacon and priest of the Anglican faith in 1852. Twenty years later he was consecrated, at Westminster Abbey, as Bishop of the diocese of Moosonee, which covered an area of fifteen hundred square miles. His account of working in the area, travelling by dogsled and canoe, is a story of dedication fraught with peril. On one trip, the birchbark canoe in which he was riding struck a rock and a large hole soon allowed the icy water to flood in. After a mad dash for the shore, the paddlers leapt to safety. Ever resourceful, they stripped bark from a birch tree and, in two hours, the canoe was made seaworthy again. On another trip Horden set off across the ice on Hannah Bay with a dog team and two guides. Seated in a carriole, he had reached the middle of Bay when one of the guides exclaimed, "The tide's coming in!" Looking seaward, the three men were horrified to see masses of ice rising and falling. The guide struck the ice with his stick and it went right through. With the end of the cariole dipping into the sea, the alert dogs sensed the danger and raced safely to the shore.

Nature was not the only threat to Horden's mission. Whooping cough swept through Moose Factory in 1883, killing forty-four people. The Horden family were not exempt: they lost an infant grandson. Starvation could be the greatest killer among the Cree and the Inuit. Horden's letters give chilling accounts of whole families being wiped out whenever there was a prolonged shortage of game and wild fowl. (A hospital for tuberculosis patients was also established in Moose Factory in more recent times. Patients were brought there from distant parts of the north. Today the 126-bed facility, with its well-insulated, overhead heating pipes, serves the people of the Hudson Bay area as a general hospital.)

When not consumed by his ministerial duties, Horden attended to the construction of a new dwelling house, a school, and a church. St. Thomas Anglican Church on Front Road in Moose Factory was built by the Hudson's Bay Company in 1864. One spring, while the church was still under construction, the settlement was visited by a disastrous flood. The water level became so high that the new church, already framed on its

St. Thomas Anglican Church, Moose Factory.

foundation, floated a quarter mile away. With the aid of ropes, pulleys, and sheer human energy, it was dragged back to its former position and then securely anchored. Again, in 1912, the church was threatened and almost floated away in the rising waters, but the inhabitants of Moose Factory managed to hold it on its foundation. To prevent a recurrence, holes, which could be plugged, were drilled into the floor, allowing water to fill the building without carrying it away.

The red-roofed white clapboard church of 1864, with its ceiling built to resemble the inside of a canoe, is still standing today. Beaded moose hides, skilfully made by local artisans, form the altar cloths and lectern hangings. Prayer books in the Cree language are still used. The pews and the pulpit have been painstakingly carved by hand. During the long summer days, sunlight streams through the stained glass windows. (In the small church cemetery there is a recent monument to the people of the area who died from tuberculosis.)

After thirty-seven years of ministering to his flock in the Moosonee diocese, Horden set out on his fourth and final visit to his old home across the ocean. He travelled by canoe to Missanabie, with his eight-year-old grandson. From here the pair went by rail to Ottawa, Montréal, and Québec City. To Horden's little grandson, all things were new and strange. When his grandfather bought an apple and an orange on the train, the little boy had to ask, "Which one is which?" They arrived in England twelve days after their departure from Québec City. Horden was reunited with his wife, who had made the trip six years earlier and remained in England. But he found that his heart was still far away across the water, amid the secluded forests of Moosonee.

He returned alone to his mission at Moose Factory. Here, during a very short illness, he finished his translation of the Bible into Cree. Then, in his mid-sixties, he died on January 12, 1893. On a beautiful, sunny afternoon, his beloved people in the Canadian north reverently buried him in the old cemetery. His large, flat-faced tombstone records some of the work accomplished by a dedicated pioneer. Braving the harsh climate, pink roses still wreath the stone, as if to pay tribute to a remarkable man.

Sadly, St. Thomas Anglican Church in Moose Factory, an important link to the most northern part of the Ontario past, will soon be closed. Requiring considerable repairs and modernization, the building will no longer be serving as a place of worship for the Cree and other people of the area. The Anglican congregation has chosen to buy a newer, more up-to-date Roman Catholic church, down the road from the old monument to the work of Bishop John Horden. At least for the time being, however, one can still visit both the old St. Thomas building of 1864 and the present Moose Factory Centennial Museum Park, and learn a little more about a part of the province that has remained quite close to the natural wilderness Horden came to love so much.

Dundas County

25. St. Peter's Evangelical Lutheran Church, 1865
Williamsburg, north of Morrisburg

Saying unto them, It is written,
My house is the house of prayer.
Luke 19:46

During the later nineteenth century, "German" was the fourth largest Old World ethnic origin in Ontario (after "Irish," "English," and, as the censuses of the day put it, "Scotch"). This story goes back at least as far as the United Empire Loyalists who arrived in what is now the eastern part of the province right after the American Revolution. A case in point is the group of twenty-five Loyalist families of German background who settled in the Williamsburg area of what later became Dundas County, Upper Canada, in July 1784. They had taken up arms in defense of the Crown during the War of Independence. For their loyalty, each family head was awarded two hundred acres of land and given provisions for their first two years.

Being of German background, these twenty-five families were also of the Lutheran faith. Like other newly arrived immigrants, they were concerned keep their religious faith alive. Every Sabbath the sound of hymns sung in German filled the air. The building of their first church began in 1788, but due to an early, severe winter, was delayed until the following spring. Called the "Dutch church" by the neighbouring English, it was identified in official records as the "German Protestant Church." A pastor, Reverend Samuel Swartfeger, was recruited from Albany, New York, to consecrate what was finally known among its members as Zion's Church — the first Lutheran church in Ontario.

The Lutheran religion stretches back to October 1517 — when Martin Luther nailed his ninety-five theses to the door of the Wittenberg Cathedral. The Protestant Reformation that followed split the Christian Church of the sixteenth century into a number of sects, of which the Lutherans were one. Luther requested his followers not call themselves Lutherans, but "Evangelicals" or believers in the gospel. But his followers did not heed his request.

St Peter's Evangelical Lutheran Church, Williamsburg.

Salvation through faith is an essential part of the Lutheran doctrine. Most Lutherans maintain that a way of living is an outgrowth of believing. They have kept the altar, cross, candles, vestments, and other earlier items of worship in their sanctuaries. The Lord's Supper, in Lutheran teaching, is an encounter with the living Lord, who is present in the Holy Communion. No physical change, however, is thought to take place in the bread and wine.

In 1793 the Lutherans of Zion's Church in the Williamsburg area of Dundas County, Upper Canada, petitioned the provincial legislature and received a grant of land, which was used for an orchard and a parsonage. In 1808, a new pastor, Reverend Weigandt, the son-in-law of Reverend Swartfeger, was called to minister to the congregation. Almost at once he changed denominations and was re-ordained into the Church of England. In attempting to convert the Lutherans to the Anglican faith, he had to contend with a wrathful, divided congregation. Although he preached in both German and English, he used only English for the prayers. Some members sided with Reverend Weigandt. Others angrily demanded that the church be turned over to those who wished to remain Lutheran. Determined to have his way, the Reverend Weigandt padlocked the door and denied the Lutherans access to the building. Because they did not have a deed to the land, a compromise was struck: it was agreed that each group would hold services on alternate Sundays.

In 1826, a new pastor, Reverend Hyunga, gathered the scattered flock together and divided it into two Lutheran groups. Under his auspices, the first church building for a new St. Peter's Lutheran congregation in Williamsburg took shape. A bargain was struck with Presbyterians in the area: they would share the costs and on alternate fortnights the new church would accommodate both Lutherans and Presbyterians. Reverend Hyunga admonished his congregation to spend their time outside the church in thanksgiving and prayer at home with their families, and to abstain from such acts of riotous living as dancing and idleness.

During the latter days of Canada West, St. Peter's Evangelical Lutheran Church in Williamsburg began to make plans for a new building of its own. The solid grey stone structure that still stands today, topped by a rudimentary tin-covered spire, was dedicated in December 1865. The site of the old church was converted to the Williamsburg (Old Union) cemetery.

Like many houses of worship across the province, St. Peter's was subsequently struck by a bolt of lightning, which ripped part of the tin from the tower. Fortunately, the building was not set alight and very little damage was done. In spite of one brother's objection that "the house was built for the worship of God" — implying that if God wanted to destroy the church He should be allowed to do so — the congregation voted to take out insurance. It proved a wise decision: more than seventy years later another bolt from the sky would smite the tower and partially burn it.

In Dundas County, as in other parts of Ontario, having a German background or name was frequently considered politically incorrect during both world wars of the twentieth century. Although some of the earliest pioneer names had already assumed an anglicized spelling, an aura of suspicion surrounded them. In order to avoid the stigma, some German families insisted that they were "Pennsylvania Dutch." In fact, thirty-nine members of St. Peter's Evangelical Lutheran Church in Williamsburg served in the Second World War, and two were killed in action.

Various changes have taken place inside the church over the years. Among other things, a chancel with three attractive Gothic arches has been installed. The end result is a pleasant interior, and a harmonious place in which to worship. To honour the present confederation's centennial in 1967, the congregation erected a base for the pole that still flies Canada's new maple leaf flag.

26. Dundela Church (Presbyterian), 1881
Dundela, northwest of Morrisburg

And out of the ground made the Lord
God to grow every tree that is pleasant
to the sight, and good for food.
Genesis 2: 9

During the earlier days of Canada West, McIntosh Corners in Dundas County, just west of Williamsburg, became more formally known as Dundela. The inhabitants were overjoyed when a post office opened in this small village in 1865. A wood frame Presbyterian church had been erected in 1832, and it would be replaced in by a new brick building in 1881. Driving along County Road 18 today, one can find neither the church nor the post office. But there is still a place to visit, in particular tribute to one of Ontario's more interesting early pioneers.

In 1796, after a family dispute, the nineteen-year-old John McIntosh moved from the famed Mohawk Valley in New York State to the southern part of Dundas County, Upper Canada. In 1811 he moved again, somewhat north, to the site of Dundela. Here he became famous in his own right as the father of the McIntosh Red apple — now enjoyed around the world.

There are two legends surrounding the birth of this distinctive fruit. One posits that an apple seedling brought by McIntosh from the United States was grafted onto a seedling found in the Dundela area. Another — promoted by the McIntosh family itself and preferred by people around Dundela today — claims that McIntosh discovered several small apple trees struggling to survive, while clearing scrub from the land he had taken up in 1811. It has been suggested that the young trees grew from apple cores tossed away by early travellers through the area. McIntosh dug the trees up and transplanted them in the garden near his house. (If we choose to believe this second legend, the seedlings would probably be descended from what French Canadians called the Fameuse apple, a variety already being cultivated in nearby Augusta Township.) Whatever the new breed's exact origins, only one of the original trees remained alive by 1830.

Although John McIntosh gets credit for rescuing and nourishing this original tree, it was his son, Allan, who established a nursery and began grafting other branches of

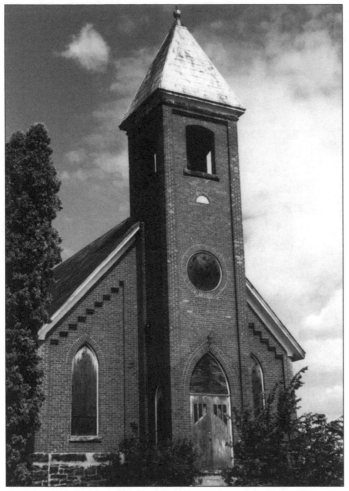

Dundela's brick church before it was torn down.

apples onto the original tree. From the seeds of this fruit other trees were grown. All who savoured the unique sweet flavour of the resulting apples urged the McIntosh family to give a name to their distinctive new product. The family combined its own surname with the brilliant red colour of the fruit to come up with the term McIntosh Red apple. Twice, at exhibitions in London, England, it would be judged the best dessert apple in the British empire.

John McIntosh himself died in 1845. But the old wood frame dwelling he had erected on his property in Dundela remained standing until 1894, when it was burned to the ground in an accidental fire. At this time the original McIntosh Red apple tree, only fifteen feet from the house, was badly scorched on one side. It would nonetheless live on and produce apples for another twelve years. A monument was erected to John McIntosh and his original tree in 1912. Today a plain stone slab marks the site where the tree flourished for ninety years. One of its scions, branches laden with fruit, arches over the monument.

Although other apples with better shipping qualities have subsequently been developed, the McIntosh Red still accounts for about a third of the total production of the crop in Ontario. No one who has bitten into a "Mac" fresh from the tree will forget its distinctive, spicy taste.

Over the years, the population of Dundela has dwindled. The brick Presbyterian church of 1881 that replaced the wood frame structure of John McIntosh's day was eventually closed. There was some controversy about its fate. Should it be torn down or restored? Then vandals broke into the church and set it ablaze. Badly damaged, the structure was finally torn down, and another part of Ontario's heritage vanished forever. All that remains of the McIntosh family's old church today is the bell from the tower, housed in a small cupola where the building once stood.

A walk through the adjacent cemetery reveals the names of McIntosh family members engraved on the tombstones. John McIntosh's name is not among them. Through a break in the trees, one may walk into a small glade. Here in an unmarked grave, in the oldest part of the cemetery, John McIntosh is buried.

A short distance away is a fruit market. On bright autumn days, bushels of glowing red apples are lined up at the roadside stand. You can still stop and sample the unsurpassed flavour of fruit descended from the original McIntosh tree.

The memorial bell in the cupola is all that remains of Dundela Presbyterian Church.

Old Ontario
(1867–1905)

The inability of predominantly French-speaking Canada East and predominantly English-speaking Canada West to live so closely together, in a single province, was one force behind the Canadian confederation of 1867. The American Civil War (1861–1865) was another, and there were others again — to the east in what is now Atlantic Canada, and to the north and west as well.

The resulting new Canada was the first self-governing dominion of the British empire. (The official name of the day, "Dominion of Canada," has now faded from regular use, but it is said to have been inspired in part by Psalm 72: "He shall have dominion also from sea to sea and from the river unto the ends of the earth.")

Along with the old United Province of Canada, the new self-governing dominion created in 1867 included the two British North American Atlantic or Maritime provinces of Nova Scotia and New Brunswick. In 1869 the federal government of the new dominion, headquartered in Ottawa, purchased the vast fur-trading territories of the north and west from the Hudson's Bay Company. On the Pacific coast the British crown colony of British Columbia joined the dominion in 1871, and Prince Edward Island did the same on the Atlantic in 1873. The larger Atlantic island of Newfoundland would remain officially undecided until 1949, but with this exception by the mid 1870s the geography of Canada as we know it today was largely in place.

The confederation of 1867 also divided the old United Province into the two new Canadian provinces of Ontario and Québec. The old separate province of Upper Canada — quite changed by the turbulent quarter-century saga of Canada West — came back to life as Ontario, already the most populous province of the new confederation. Toronto was its capital, and John Sandfield Macdonald (no relation to Canada's first federal prime minister, Sir John A. Macdonald) was its first premier.

"Sandfield Macdonald" was an interesting man, whose accomplishments included a stylish French-speaking wife from Louisiana. But he was getting older, and his so-called "Patent Combination" government was short-lived. The much more important figure for the future of Ontario would be Oliver Mowat, elected and re-elected provincial premier without interruption for almost a quarter of a century, from 1872 to 1896. A stern, shrewd, and staunch Presbyterian who "wore the white flower of a blameless life," Mowat believed deeply in the importance of religion and the local church for the rising provincial society. For his day, he was also quite ecumenical and broad-minded. As he explained to some critics in the 1880s: "I would not be fit for my official position if I did not feel and know that a man may be a true Protestant without hating or ostracizing Roman Catholics ... . I have endeavoured to show to our mixed community that an earnest, fair-minded Protestant premier may be true to his Protestantism, and yet be entitled to the reasonable confidence of thinking Roman Catholics."

The Old Ontario era of Oliver Mowat, in the later nineteenth century, was the great golden age of the family farm in the province. The primitive pioneering frontier was moving to the north and west. Southern Ontario had become a place of established farm communities and supporting towns and villages, linked by water routes, railways, and still quite rugged but symmetrically laid-out roads. Agriculture, supplemented by lumbering, was the mainstay of the provincial economy. The majority of the population would continue to live, work, and worship in rural areas until just before the First World War.

At the same time, beneath the surface of the rural mainstream, a new kind of urban life had already begun to arise in the province's growing cities, with its own new pioneers. Ontario agricultural machinery manufactured by the enterprises of the Massey and Harris families was starting to find markets in places beyond Canada. Timothy Eaton had begun to build a commercial empire of up-to-date department stores, and the Canadian Bank of Commerce was pioneering Toronto's role as a rising financial centre.

Meanwhile, Ned Hanlan from Toronto became the rowing champion of the world in 1880. Adelaide Hoodless founded the first Women's Institute at Stoney Creek, Ontario, in 1897 — a model for a movement that would soon spread across Canada and around the world. The old first peoples' game of lacrosse was more popular than it has subsequently become, but the related game of ice hockey had started its long development as Canada's ultimate national sport. (The Stanley Cup was first won in 1893, by a team from Montréal: it would take another decade for the Ottawa Silver Seven to bring it to Ontario for the first time, in 1903.)

The earlier rapid pace of Ontario's population growth slowed down somewhat for a time, giving the new province a chance to consolidate the now very vast changes that had transformed the landscape since the late eighteenth century. By the late nineteenth century, another buoyant wave of new arrivals had started — from Great Britain and other increasingly more diverse places across the sea. New places of worship continued to dot the countryside and the rising cities. Oliver Mowat's mixed community continued to take its various religions very seriously.

Frontenac County

27. Christ Church, Cataraqui (Anglican), 1870
974 Sydenham Road, Kingston

> *I am like those who hear me,*
> *a Canadian heart and soul.*
> Sir John A. Macdonald (1815–1891)

*N*ow more than a century and a quarter old, Christ Church, Cataraqui, in the outer reaches of the present-day City of Kingston, has the singular honour of being surrounded by Cataraqui Cemetery, which hosts the grave site of the man who was the first prime minister and, in at least some respects, the chief architect of the new confederation of 1867.

A wrought-iron fence encloses the modest plot where Sir John A. Macdonald lies today. The Canada of the present is not exactly what he had in mind — thanks in no small part to his one real rival in the later nineteenth century, the premier of Ontario, Sir Oliver Mowat. But the Canada that still stretches from the Atlantic to the Arctic to the Pacific Oceans does owe a great deal to Sir John A. (and to his original French Canadian partner, Georges Étienne Cartier). This particular Macdonald had much to do with the creation of the new dominion in 1867, and he served as its prime minister from 1867 until 1873, and then again from 1878 until his death in 1891. It was his wily, dogged determination that finally led to the completion of the Canadian Pacific Railway, linking the new country from sea to sea, in 1885.

John Alexander, second son of the ambitious but feckless Hugh Macdonald and the intelligent

Sir John A. Macdonald's grave,
Cataraqui Cemetery.

and capable Helen Shaw, was born on January 10 (or some say 11), 1815, in Glasgow, Scotland. In the summer of 1820, the five-year-old boy, with his parents, his younger brother, and two sisters, immigrated to Kingston in Upper Canada.

With a face that might have been hewn from rugged Scottish granite, the adult John Alexander Macdonald would be noted for his bright eye, a lively wit, and a countenance as fluid as the liquid comfort he always kept on hand. His wide, sensuous mouth, tucked at the corners, was ever ready to break into a smile. His most famous feature, his overly large spade-like nose, was described by one biographer as "designed as much for digging as for sniffing."

Family tragedy was common enough in the nineteenth-century, and the Macdonald family was no exception. An older brother, William, had died at an early age — before the trip across the ocean. An unfortunate incident subsequently took the life of John Alexander's younger brother in Upper Canada. Not yet six years old, he was struck a brutal blow by his father's assistant and fell with such force that he was fatally injured. (The adult John A. would have his own share of such grief, with a first son who died at thirteen months, a first wife who was an invalid for most of the marriage, and a chronically ill daughter from his second marriage.)

Soon after the death of the younger brother, the Macdonald family moved to the Bay of Quinte, within sight of the Hay Bay Church, where they lived in an old red clapboard house. Here, the young John A. attended a primitive school at Adolphustown. A dour, elderly gentleman remembered only as Old Hughes presided over not only the young boy's education but over his moral training as well. For the many tricks he played, John Alexander had his behind soundly whacked by Old Hughes. Although not athletically inclined, the young Macdonald was considered fleet of foot and a good runner (qualities which would also serve him well in his later political life). In the speeches of his later years, he would describe the pleasure he had derived from running barefoot during his all-too-brief, carefree childhood summers at Hay Bay.

Once again the family moved, this time from Hay Bay to Glenora. Because there was no school in the area, John Alexander was sent to Kingston to complete his education. Then, at fourteen, his school days were over; the rest of his education would be in the world of experience. At fifteen, having passed the admission examinations to Osgoode Hall, he apprenticed with a law office in Kingston. Six years later he received his law degree, and his long career in law, business, and especially politics was launched.

It may say something about what John A. Macdonald became in Canada that he was a Scotsman who lies buried in a cemetery that surrounds an Anglican church. The history of Anglican worship in the Cataraqui area of present-day Kingston dates back as far as 1835, and the first church rectory had been constructed in 1859 by inmates of

Christ Church, Cataraqui, Kingston.

Kingston Penitentiary. But it wasn't until three years after confederation, in 1870, that the building of the present Christ Church took place.

Like the Macdonald family, this beautiful limestone structure has had its tragedies. In 1922 the congregation installed electricity and, in the same year lightning, whether ordained by God or inspired by Lucifer, struck the tower and ripped off the stone on the southeast corner. The mighty blast demolished two pews and smashed a hole in the floor. The church was visited by another tragedy in 1981, when fire destroyed the vaulted ceiling and the wood panelling on the inside walls. Many of the stained glass windows were damaged or destroyed. The renovated interior is a less ornate but just as vital environment. Although his opposition would have no doubt wished to give him credit, Christ Church does not hold Sir John A. responsible for these disasters.

On June 11, 1891, thousands of people on foot and in almost every kind of vehicle then extant followed the body of Sir John A. Macdonald over the dusty road to Cataraqui Cemetery. Almost seventy-three years since he had first stepped onto the dock at Kingston, Sir John A. was interred beside the graves of his parents, his first wife, and their infant son.

Whatever else might be said, only a few others have given as much of their time and energy in service to the people of Canada. Some words from one of his addresses sum up an immigrant's devotion and dedication to his new country: "And though I have the misfortune ... to be a Scotsman ... my affections, my family are here. All my hopes and remembrances are Canadian; and not only are my principles and prejudices Canadian, but my interests are Canadian. I am like those who hear me, a Canadian, heart and soul."

From the grassy knoll in Cataraqui Cemetery today, beside the modest monument, one can hear the hum of traffic from the Macdonald-Cartier Freeway (as Ontario's Highway 401 is now officially known, in honour of Sir John A. and his French-Canadian partner of the confederation era). Some considerable distance due north, along the banks of the Ottawa River, runs the main line of the Canadian Pacific Railway that first united Canada from sea to sea — realizing at least some important parts of Macdonald's nineteenth-century dream for a new Canadian future.

Wellington County

28. St. John the Evangelist Anglican Church, 1873
41 Church Street, Elora, northwest of Guelph

Long has the night of sorrow reigned:
The dawn shall bring us light.
"Come Let Us to the God of Love,"
Voices United, Hymn #653

Sir John A. Macdonald bumped into his first big patch of trouble as prime minister of Canada in the fall of 1873, when scandalous allegations surrounding the early construction of the Canadian Pacific Railway forced his resignation from office. The present building of St. John the Evangelist Anglican Church in the village of Elora, Wellington County, Ontario, was constructed in the same year — of sturdy red brick, and with an almost free-standing steepled tower.

In fact, the congregation of St. John the Evangelist in Elora dates back to 1842, when its original wood frame building, modelled after a little church in Conway, Wales, had been consecrated. The church's early history also holds the legend of a famous woman of the British empire and her adoring lover. The legend began when, in his declining years, the Reverend John Smithhurst revealed to a friend the name of the great love of his life: Florence Nightingale.

There can be little doubt that the Reverend Smithhurst was deeply enamoured with Florence and, eschewing marriage and children, remained true to this love all the days of his life. But was the "Lady with a Lamp" ever really in love with John Smithhurst? It was only when he was an elderly, ailing man that John told the startling story of his love for Florence, and how she had decided that being first cousins was an insuperable obstacle to any union between them. Although it is understandable that such a marriage would prompt social disapproval, it would not have been illegal or unprecedented.

At the time, Florence, still in her late teens, was perhaps not above indulging in a number of flirtations, and she may have had a fleeting dalliance with her cousin, twelve years her senior. Yet she was a strong-minded woman who, in spite of all her parents' protestations, took up a nursing career then considered eminently unsuitable for a young

St. John the Evangelist Anglican Church, Elora.

lady of her position. In order to fulfil what she saw as her destiny, she was finally forced to divorce herself completely from her family. (In her notes of 1837, she likens her experience to that of Joan of Arc: "God spoke to me and called me to his service.") If such a determined woman had truly loved John Smithhurst, would she ever be persuaded by her protesting family to cast her love aside, merely to avoid social disapproval?

According to his own testimony, John had asked Florence to marry him and, when she refused, he said, "Florence, if you do not marry me, what am I to do?" She replied, "John, I would like you to be a missionary to the Indians in North America." Was this Florence's way of gently saying "no" to a person whom she may have liked very much but did not love deeply?

Florence Nightingale's refusal of his marriage proposal, in any case, marked a turning point in John Smithhurst's life. He gave up his business career and entered the church. In 1839, he was ordained by the Bishop of London and immediately set sail for the Red River settlement in present-day Manitoba, where he became the first exclusively Anglican missionary to the Red River Cree. Like many such figures, he lived through his share of great privations and sacrifices. In his diary, he records that, in what we now know as the bitterly cold Winnipeg winter, his shoes froze to the stirrups and his horse, white with frost, had icicles hanging from its mouth. In summer he was so plagued by mosquitoes that he longed for the return of winter.

While the Reverend Smithhurst lovingly shared his life with the Red River Cree, Florence Nightingale would devote her life to her one true love: the improvement of nursing care for the British soldier, in times of both war and peace.

In 1851, John made a final journey to England, still hoping to marry Florence. During the intervening years, she had had several offers of marriage — among them one from a Richard Moncton Milnes who was considered a very eligible bachelor. Upon refusing Milnes, she wrote, "I could be satisfied to spend a life with the man I adored in combining our different powers in some great object. I could not satisfy this nature by spending a life with him in making society and arranging domestic things." Had she truly adored John Smithhurst, could she not have been partners with him in his great object of ministering to the Red River Cree?

Upon the subsequent marriage of Richard Moncton Milnes to another, Miss Nightingale also recorded in her notes, "Lastly all my admirers are married ... and I stand with the world before me." Did she not consider John Smithhurst one of her admirers? He was still unmarried and, in later years, by his own confession, still very much in love with the aloof Florence.

In 1852, despondent over his continuing failure to win Florence Nightingale's hand, John Smithhurst sailed again for Canada, where he became the rector of St. John the Evangelist Church in Elora, in the rising Canada West. He would not live to see the construction of the present church building in 1873. But in a special vault in the wall, to the right of the present chancel, there is still a communion set with the following inscription: "Acting as agent for someone, Ebenezer Hall gave as a gift, this set of communion silver to Reverend John Smithhurst, a very dear friend, in grateful recognition of his many acts of kindness. A.D. 1852." Did Florence give the service to John as a token of love, or just as a gesture of friendship to someone dear to her? Only she could know what affection was in her heart. And each time the Reverend Smithhurst raised the communion cup to his lips saying, "Do this in remembrance of me," did the name of his beloved Florence echo in his mind?

Grown old beyond his fifty-nine years, the Reverend John Smithhurst died in the year of Canadian confederation, 1867. Standing by his lonely grave in the cemetery of St. John the Evangelist in Elora today, one can hear the distant roar of the Grand and Irvine Rivers where they conjoin and tumble down a deep gorge, much as he must have heard long ago. Across the ocean, more than forty years after Smithhurst's death, Florence Nightingale, scorning the offer of a burial in Westminster Abbey, expressed a wish that "no memorial should mark the place where lies my Mortal Coil." In deference to her wishes, she was buried in the family plot at East Wellow. Her only memorial is one line on the family tombstone: "F. N. Born 1820. Died 1910."

Back in Old Ontario, when the members of St. John the Evangelist in Elora had dedicated two stained glass windows in the sanctuary of their new building of 1873, they apparently believed that they were honouring the memory of two star-crossed lovers. Imprisoned in separate windows are the solitary figures of the Reverend John Smithhurst and his beloved Florence Nightingale — who remain apart here as surely as they did in real life, the true secret of their love known only to themselves.

For many years after the deaths of both John and Florence, on the third Sunday in October, nurses in spotless uniforms gathered in holy fellowship at St. John the Evangelist Anglican Church in Elora to honour the Lady with a Lamp, who devoted her entire adult life to easing the sufferings of others. The church is still known today as the "Nurses' Shrine."

Northumberland County

29. Canton United Church, 1876
Canton, north of Welcome

John Brown's body lies a-mouldering in the grave ...
But his Soul goes marching on!
Glory! Glory! Hallelujah ... .
"John Brown's Body," American Civil War Song

The American Civil War helped bring about the Canadian confederation of 1867. It also had some more direct impact on the lives of people in the new Canadian province of Ontario, and some of this can still be seen at Canton United Church in Northumberland County.

Although the present church building dates back to 1876, Hope Chapel, constructed in the once-flourishing village of Canton in 1831, was the first place of worship erected by the predominantly Methodist population of the area. One tends to regard Methodists as no-nonsense people, but when Hope Chapel got underway in Canton there was a joyous celebration. After the laying of the cornerstone, the congregation retired to Beechwood, the spacious home of one of the members where swings for children, lawn croquet, and other popular amusements were provided. Then the Port Hope Band played in nearby Welcome. A charge of twenty-five cents per person was adequate for the tea, strawberries, and cream which completed the celebrations.

The old chapel building of 1831 has survived alongside the present Canton United Church of 1876. With assistance from Vincent Massey, who became Canada's first Canadian-born governor general in 1952, it has been converted into a community hall. (Vincent Massey was also a descendant of the agricultural machinery family, which has some of its nineteenth-century roots in this particular part of Ontario.) Although many alterations were made to the chapel when it became a community hall, the original domed ceiling and gallery have been retained.

Of pleasing appearance, the present red brick church, with its soaring steeple, is a replica of a sister church in nearby Port Hope. The entrance has unusual side-pocket and overhead doors that can be opened to give greater access to the attractive, vaulted interior.

Seats recessed in the sides of the ornate wrought-iron pews were extended to accommodate the high levels of church attendance in Old Ontario. All that remains of the once-bustling community of Canton today are the community hall, which used to be Hope Chapel, and the present red brick church — standing in isolated splendor across the road from the Canton cemetery.

One of the most beautiful rural burying grounds in Ontario, the Canton cemetery dates back to 1811 when Susan Hawkins, the young wife of James Hawkins, was the first interment in the south end of the then private burial ground. The passing of the years has almost obliterated the inscription on the small headstone that marks her grave.

The cemetery is entered through wrought-iron gates. Reminiscent of an English country graveyard, a double row of pyramidal cedars forms a shaded walkway for the entire length of the cemetery. Tall, spreading maples shelter the graves from the summer sun. Many of the tombstones bear the names of infants and children, silent testimony to the high mortality rate among the young in earlier times. Facing towards heaven, one endearing stone is in the shape of a small, sleeping cherub whose slumber has been undisturbed by the passing of the years.

Walking into the cemetery, one can't miss the monument and plaque on the right side of the path, in honour of Edward E. Dodds, who fought on the side of the Union Army during the American Civil War. Though the hard evidence for the often-noted estimates of as many as 40,000 to 50,000 such men is still in question, it is clear enough that more than a few young Canadians

Canton United Church.

or British North Americans took part in the Civil War. Some were no doubt lured by rest-lessness and vague prospects of financial gain. Others enlisted out of genuine commitment to what *The Globe* of the day in Toronto had called "the noble trust of shielding free institutions." (Considerably smaller numbers again actually fought for the Confederacy.)

While still a teenager, Edward Dodds from Northumberland County, on the north shore of Lake Ontario, had enlisted with the 21st New York Cavalry, across the lake in Rochester. On July 19, 1864, at Ashby's Gap near Winchester, Virginia, Dodds risked his life to rescue his wounded captain and carry him from the fury and hell of the battlefield. For this brave action he was subsequently awarded the U.S. Congressional Medal of Honour.

Some Canadians who fought in the American Civil War would remain in the United States when the war ended. Edward Dodds returned to Northumberland County, Ontario — missing an arm that he lost either at Ashby's Gap in 1864, or in some other part of the struggle. In the heyday of Old Ontario he and his sons are reported to have been local licence brokers in Port Hope, who also published a directory of Northumberland and Durham Counties in the 1880s. Today Edward Dodds lies in the Canton cemetery beneath a monument to his youthful military heroism. It took only fifty years for admirers walking barefoot and singing the John Brown story (John Brown's song) to recognize John Brown's heroic martyrdom. But it would take 120 years before Civil War buffs would recall Edward E. Dodds' daring exploit and install a worthy monument to him. Firmly planted in the earth in front of the monument, a small star-spangled banner droops in remembrance of a Canadian who risked everything to pre-serve the Union and make all its people free.

Near the hamlet of Welcome, just north of Port Hope, the Canton cemetery and the Canton United Church are attractively located among Northumberland County's rolling hills. The cemetery overlooks a small branch of the Ganaraska River which leisurely wends its way to Lake Ontario. One ideal time to visit is in the autumn, when spreading maples become torches of brilliant colour. Equally delightful is a drive along the Canton Road in spring, when the roadsides and the fields adjoining the cemetery are a palette of purple and white lilacs. Like the original celebrants of Hope Chapel, present-day church members still hold a strawberry festival each year in June.

Hastings County

30. St. Peter's Presbyterian Church, 1877
115 St. Lawrence Street West, Madoc

Greater love hath no man than this,
that a man lay down his life for his friends.
John 15:13

Considered somewhat common in style, the original St. Peter's Presbyterian Church in Madoc, Hastings County (just east of Northumberland) was built in 1850. Although a spiritual fire had been kindled in the hearts of the congregation to build a bigger and better sanctuary, it would take an actual inferno to sweep the little church away. The cry "Fire" roused the citizens of the small village one night in May 1873. The blaze had already levelled nearly the entire business section. Because the church was on an elevation of land some distance from the fire, it was believed to be out of the danger zone. But a strong east wind carried sparks onto the wooden roof and, before it was noticed, the church was ablaze.

The presiding minister, Reverend David Wishart, saw that his home was in the fire's direct path. He immediately dropped to his knees and prayed, "Lord, spare my house and I will raise one to your glory." In minutes, as if in answer to his prayer, the wind turned and his home remained unscathed. Plans for the building of a new church were soon made. The community regarded the new sanctuary as a direct answer to prayer and a monument to a vow fulfilled.

In June of 1874, a solid silver trowel was used to lay the cornerstone of the new church, to be built on a plot of donated land. A facsimile of Smiths Falls Presbyterian Church in Lanark County, some distance east, the door to the new St. Peter's Presbyterian in Madoc would be through the 120-foot, square clock tower. Stonemasons were brought from Scotland to work the hard grey and light brown limestone taken from a nearby quarry. Heavy wooden beams, obtained from a local farm, were needed to support the coloured slate roof. A winding staircase from the main entrance in the clock tower led to the gallery.

The stonemasons from Scotland notwithstanding, the mid-1870s parishioners of St.

Peter's were expected to donate one day's work per week until the new church was completed. They were also asked to give an extra freewill offering every Sunday. The generous and hardworking members of the congregation finally moved into their partially finished church in 1877.

One Sunday afternoon, twenty years after the inauguration of the second St. Peter's, another fire struck. The local fire brigade was quickly in position at the bridge but, unfortunately, the hoses could not reach the building, so the pail brigade took over. Realizing that this system was not fast enough, the fire brigade teams brought the engine closer to the church, and drew water in barrels to fill the pumper. The local Roman Catholic priest, Father Davis, called to the volunteers, "Boys, save the tower."

In spite of the valiant efforts of the entire village, the church was reduced to smoke-blackened walls rising out of a still-smouldering base-ment. Only the tower escaped

St. Peter's Presbyterian Church, Madoc.

destruction. Not daunted by their misfortune, the congregation immediately set about rebuilding their church. Six months after the opening service at the rebuilt structure, the Reverend David Wishart's forty-year pastorate came to an end.

Like many other rural areas of Old Ontario, Madoc in Hastings County was an incubator for some exceptional people. With a minister of David Wishart's high moral standards in the pulpit of St. Peter's Presbyterian for so many years, it is not surprising that this small village would eventually give the province one of its most notable military heroes of the Second World War.

Having grown up in St. Peter's in Madoc, John Weir Foote would go on to become a Presbyterian minister himself. During all the wars in which Canada was involved between 1854 and 1945, Captain Foote was the only member of the Canadian Chaplain Service to be awarded the Victoria Cross. No run-of-the-mill padre, he asked to be included in the daring but ill-fated Dieppe Raid of 1942. When his request was denied, he informed his superior officer that he would disobey orders and go anyway. Finally, he was assigned to the Hamilton Light Infantry as a stretcher bearer.

The Hamilton Light Infantry was one of two battalions involved in the main assault on White Beach on August 19. While the battle was in progress, John Foote assisted the medical officer attending the wounded. Under relentless fire, he was able to carry thirty wounded back to the first aid post during the next six hours. Encumbered by his heavy, wet army boots, he took them off. During the evacuation he helped carry the wounded aboard the landing craft. One of the last to leave the beach, he grabbed a Bren gun and fired at the enemy to protect his comrades in the boats. Then, seeing that there were still many wounded Canadians abandoned on the battlefield, he leaped overboard and joined the soon-to-be prisoners still on the beach. (Of the 5000 Canadians who participated in the Dieppe Raid, 900 were killed, 1000 were wounded, and nearly 2000 were taken prisoner. The rest barely managed to return to Britain.)

Having surrendered to the enemy, Foote walked barefoot along a cinder-strewn railway track for the next two days. Taken to a camp for officers, he arranged to be sent to a camp for the ranks. Known only as Padre X, he became a legend among the soldiers for the comfort and hope he gave them. He organized his own "congregation" within the camp, and it was not until he returned to Canada that he learned he had been awarded a Victoria Cross. With a record of more Victoria Crosses per capita than any other Commonwealth nation, Canada could take more pride than it often does in its military heroes. Today Captain John Weir Foote lies buried in Union Cemetery in Cobourg, southwest of Madoc.

Almost two decades before Captain Foote's acts of heroism at Dieppe, in June 1925, when the time came to vote on church union with the Methodists and Congregationalists, the Presbyterian General Assembly in Canada resolved that any congregation voting against union could remain Presbyterian. In spite of strong appeals for union, the members of St. Peter's in Madoc, Hastings County, Ontario, were among those who chose to carry on with the old faith. The present-day church remains within the Presbyterian fold.

31. Actinolite United Church, reconstructed 1889
Actinolite, Municipality of Tweed

Ye also, as lively stones, are built up a spiritual
house, an holy priesthood, to offer up spiritual
sacrifices, acceptable to God by Jesus Christ.
I Peter 2:5

A short distance east of Madoc, the present-day hamlet of Actinolite is no longer what it was in the agrarian golden age of Old Ontario. But its beautiful white marble church has endured as a monument to its people, then and now.

Nestled in the bend of the bubbling Skootamatta River, Actinolite began in the mid-1850s as a small settlement called Troy, subsequently renamed Bridgewater. Its initial driving force was the long-lived Hastings County business leader, Billa Flint (1805–1904), who established a saw mill, general store, and crusher to recover gold in the place.

In the mid 1860s, with the discovery of the mineral actinolite in the adjacent area (used in the manufacture of roofing material), Bridgewater embarked on a generation of local prosperity and population growth. Considered a model rising community of its type, it erected a model church in 1866 — on a well-chosen site south of the settlement, on the road to Belleville. Probably the only one of its kind in Canada, the Wesleyan Methodist Church in Bridgewater was built of rough-hewn white marble from a nearby quarry. Perhaps to be in tune with the white marble, the architect, Augustus J. Stapley of Belleville, designed it in the Italianate style. A fine-toned bell, made locally, was installed in the hundred-foot tower.

Over the next two decades or so, life in the model community was a pleasant experience. Thanks in no small part to the actinolite mining in the area, the people prospered and faithfully attended their church. Then, in May 1889, disaster struck. A fire broke out in the boarding house run by Mrs. Chase and her sister, Miss Clapp. According to local reports, a drunken boarder fell asleep and his pipe went unattended. The fire quickly spread to nearby buildings, almost wiping out the entire community. The beautiful marble church, in the path of the fire, was completely gutted. In the end only the stained glass windows and the marble walls (which had been constructed to resist such an event)

Actinolite's reconstructed white marble church.

remained intact.

Very few other buildings in the place had escaped the raging inferno. The suddenly impoverished residents of Bridgewater debated whether they could afford to save their church, or whether they would have to tear it down. The only insurance on the structure, $2000, was insufficient to repair the damage. Fortunately, residents of the larger metropolis of Belleville, down the road, came to the rescue. With additional help from Elzevir Township council, closer to home, enough funds were realized to restore the marble church to its original beauty. Today this pristine building still refutes all those who say, "It can't be done." In spite of their own personal losses, the undaunted people of Bridgewater had the faith and courage to return their beautiful church to its place in the community.

Bridgewater itself did not quite recover from its great fire of 1889. It was renamed Actinolite in 1895, but Actinolite never regained the prosperity and growth it had known under its former name, in the first generation of the Canadian confederation. When the United Church of Canada was formed in 1925, the old Wesleyan Methodist church became Actinolite United Church — now officially a part of the Municipality of Tweed. It is still a beautiful marble church, and a remarkable feature of the Hastings County countryside.

The Blue Church, on Highway 2 west of Prescott, is one of the most photographed churches in Ontario. Barbara Heck is buried in the adjacent cemetery. (See page 53.)

Many artists — including three members of the Group of Seven — combined their talents to create this huge dome of colour inside St. Anne's Anglican Church, in Toronto. (See page 127.)

A ceremony taking place inside Richmond Hill's warm and welcoming Hindu Temple Society of Canada. The temple is open every day. (See page 169.)

St. Thomas Anglican Church in Shanty Bay is a stucco structure that was built with a material known as "rammed earth." (See page 45.)

The above photo was taken during a regular service at the Gurdwara Shromani Sikh Society on Pape Avenue in Toronto. The colourful clothing and decorations help break up the stark interior of this converted house.
(See page 165.)

This beautiful statue stands off to one side, away from the main altar, in Hoa Nghiem Buddhist Temple on Gerrard Street in Toronto.
(See page 180.)

Toronto's Calvary Baptist Church has a special stained-glass window. This "living memorial" is made up of pieces taken from dozens of European churches destroyed during the Second World War. The full window is on the left; on the right, a closer look. (See page 145.)

The congregation of St. John the Evangelist Anglican Church in Elora believed that Reverend John Smithhurst, their minister, and Florence Nightingale were star-crossed lovers. They are separated in these two stained-glass windows, just as they were in real life. (See page 93.)

This stained-glass window in Christ the King Cathedral in Moosonee, shows the Nativity scene with a First Nations Holy Family. (See page 155.)

St. Brendan's Roman Catholic Church, in Rockport, is built on
solid rock and overlooks the St. Lawrence River. The church is
named after the patron saint of sailors. (See page 117.)

The oil motif of this stained-glass window in Petrolia's Christ Church commemorates the industry upon which the town was built. (See page 159.)

This impressive mosaic of five million tile pieces adorns the domed ceiling of Markham's Cathedral of the Transfiguration. The figure appears to be floating on air and the outstretched arms welcome all who enter the cathedral. (See page 173.)

York Region

32. St. George's Anglican Church, 1877
408 Hedge Road, Sutton (next to Sibbald Point Provincial Park)

And there was built a memory in stone
Georgina's Church, for England and St. George.
Sir Gerald Dodson (1884–1966)

Those who had wanted to see the Church of England established as the official religion of Upper Canada were not as influential in the province of Ontario created by the 1867 confederation as they had been in the earlier nineteenth century. But their influence lived on in more subtle ways. One witness to the trend is St. George's Anglican Church at Sutton, in the present-day York Region. Partly hidden from the road by pines and cedars today, it sits on a high bank overlooking a beautiful bay on Lake Simcoe. Screened by a natural growth of trees, only the Norman tower can be seen by travellers on the lake.

In the old Upper Canada the surrounding area had attracted many former half-pay personnel from the British army. Although life is never easy for any pioneers, these people fared better than many other immigrants of the day. They were modestly well-to-do and brought with them a particular set of middle-class values and expectations.

In 1835, a newly arrived middle-aged woman of just this sort had taken a steamboat ride around Lake Simcoe. Susan Sibbald, wife of an ailing Scottish colonel and mother of eleven children, had arrived in the area by ox cart to check up on two of her sons who had been shipped out to the new frontier. William and Charles Sibbald had found lodging in a local tavern. When word of their dwelling place reached their horrified parents in Scotland, Mr. And Mrs. Sibbald feared that their sons would become debauched. Although it meant leaving behind an ailing husband, it was decided that Mrs. Sibbald, accompanied by another son, would travel to Upper Canada to rescue William and Charles.

When she arrived, Mrs. Sibbald was so entranced by the beauty of the southern shore of Lake Simcoe that she decided to purchase a four-hundred-acre shoreline property that was up for sale. Upon completion of the deal, she renamed the existing house on the property Eildon Hall, after her ancestral home at the foot of the Eildon Hills in Scotland.

In fact, "tavern" in Upper Canada had a different connotation from that to which Susan Sibbald was accustomed, and she discovered that her sons were living exemplary lives. The first thing this righteous woman, nonetheless, did was demolish a tavern located on her own new estate. Her second undertaking was the building of a church. This first Anglican place of worship in the area was a modest wooden structure whose entranceway was through a steepled tower. Coming from a British military family, the colonel's wife insisted that the newly built church be named for St. George, the soldier saint of England. Members of the Sibbald family had served in the armed forces of the empire since the Napoleonic Wars. In Upper Canada, Canada West, and Ontario they would carry on with the tradition, through the Rebellion of 1837, the so-called Fenian Raids at the end of the American Civil War, and both world wars of the twentieth century. (Four Sibbalds have died while serving their country.)

The only Anglican church for miles around, the opening of the original St. George's at Sutton was a day of rejoicing. Some of the older folk had not been in a church for many years, and most of the children born in the area had never seen the inside of one. Prayers of thankfulness were offered and hymns of praise and joy were sung.

Unlike many of her fellow early pioneers, who would never again see their homeland, Susan Sibbald, coming from a family of substance, was able to travel back to Britain, where she lived again for a period of time. But upon the death of her husband, she returned to Canada where she settled into her home on Lake Simcoe. She found both Eildon Hall and St. George's Church badly dilapidated. One of her dreams had been to build a more substantial church to replace the old wood-frame structure. At the age of eighty-three, she died before she could realize the dream, and was buried in a family plot in the churchyard.

In the 1870s her three sons in the area undertook the building of a new stone church as a memorial to their mother. The old church was rolled off the site and the building of the new one began. A former commander in the British Navy, Thomas Sibbald took charge of the work. He operated on meticulous military routine. Following strict naval procedure, every worker was expected to be on the job each day at eight bells, when he would be given a tot of rum. In order to prevent any flawed stones from being used in the construction, Captain Thomas inspected each one, and rejected the hard granite blocks containing traces of iron. One small, rectangular stone, saturated with iron, escaped Captain Thomas's notice and was incorporated into the building, which was finally completed in 1877. This rust-stained stone, about six feet from the

St. George's Anglican Church, Sutton.

ground at the west end of the church, can still be seen bleeding onto the stones below. The only mark of imperfection on an otherwise perfectly pristine building, one can only surmise that someone thought the perfection needed to be offset with a blemish.

Rather than move them, the graves of several people were left undisturbed beneath the foundation of the present church. An inscription to their memory was set into the wall of the building. On the west side of the church tower, a marble tablet commemorates the tragic death of Charles Sibbald's wife and daughter, who were burned to death when the steamship *Bavarian*, travelling from Toronto to Montréal, caught fire and burned on Lake Ontario.

The interior of the church today is pleasingly simple in design. Much of the wood used is black walnut and butternut. Upon close inspection, one can find a beaver motif (the emblem of the fur trade) carved in the wood of the easternmost arch on the right side. One feature that captures a visitor's eye immediately is the stained-glass window depicting St. George slaying the dragon — a symbol said to represent victory over tyranny and right over might. A more recent addition to the building, this window has been appropriately dedicated to members of the congregation who were killed in the two world wars.

The east window, located above the altar, was removed from the old wooden building for installation in the new stone church. The seven-cross motif in the central panel is a reference to the seven daughters of Upper Canada's first lieutenant governor, John Graves Simcoe (whose memory also lives on in the name Lake Simcoe). The motif was apparently designed and hand-coloured by Simcoe's daughters, back in Great Britain.

No visit to St. George's at Sutton would be complete without a stroll through the churchyard, where visitors can pause to read the tombstone inscriptions of two famous literary personages. Stephen Leacock, still often considered Canada's greatest humorist, is buried there, a simple piece of granite marking his grave. A more imposing Celtic cross marks the grave of Mazo de la Roche, author of the very popular *Jalna* series of books (which have inspired both a Canadian television series and a Hollywood movie).

The land in the churchyard sweeps down to the lake and, through the trees, one can glimpse the loveliness of the bay with Georgina Island in the background. A stone bench on the rise of land overlooking the lake invites the casual visitor to pause and enjoy the tranquility of the scene. Passing from the churchyard to the parking lot, one should stop for a last look up at the Norman tower, where delightful gargoyles appear ready to spurt water onto the unwary visitor below.

District of Parry Sound

33. Sand Lake Pioneer Church, 1884
Sand Lake, Town of Kearney

Oh come come come come
Come to the church in the wildwood,
Oh come to the church in the vale;
No place is so dear to my childhood
As the little brown church in the vale.

William S. Pitts (1830–1918)

With the southern part of the province already largely settled, the immediate new frontier for Old Ontario was to the north. Today, the well-preserved pioneer log church at Sand Lake in the District of Parry Sound — about an hour's drive north of the most northerly reaches of Lake Simcoe — is one of the few such buildings that remain in the province. Originally located in a land of dense forest, the present-day primitive church and pioneer cemetery are in a small clearing, a short distance from the lake. A narrow dirt road wends its way past the church to the cottages that rim the shore.

Samuel de Champlain's assistant, Étienne Brûlé, who was probably the first European to set foot inside what is now Ontario, in 1610, was also probably the first person from across the ocean to see the little gem of Sand Lake. Earlier on, it is thought, there had been an Algonquin settlement near the lake. The first European building in the area was a so-called flying post, where itinerant trappers traded their furs. By the middle of the nineteenth century the fur trade had been supplanted by the logging industry. Subsequent new pioneer settlers tried their hand at farming, but this never quite worked out on land dominated by the rocky Canadian Shield. All these industries are now gone, replaced by the influx of a new kind of settler: the cottager.

In the more northerly parts of the province as elsewhere, the two things pioneers wanted most when they first settled in an area were a school and a building where they could meet on the Sabbath to worship their God. The mostly Presbyterian settlers around Sand Lake in the later nineteenth century were determined to have a place of worship. An acre of land was donated by one of the pioneer families and the building

Sand Lake Pioneer Church, Kearney.

was planned. In 1884, as the work began, the ring of axes filled the air. Cut from the nearby bush, the logs were drawn by oxen to the site. They were then hewn by broad axe and left to cure. The process required a lot of skill as the logs had to be of more or less uniform dimensions. One of the oxen drivers was a fifteen-year-old girl who, it is recorded, worked in bare feet.

A building bee was organized, and the whole community took part in the labour. Corners required particular skill as the logs had to be cut in such a way as to tie into each other. Cut from virgin timber, the pine logs are of such size that, excluding the foundation piece, it took only seven logs to form each wall.

The furnishings for the church were made from local wood by two English carpenters who lived south of Sand Lake. When the pulpit and pews were finished, they had to be transported across the lake by raft. Halfway across, the bindings of the raft loosened and the precious cargo was about to float away. A boater came to the aid of the rafters and managed to get them safely to shore. Getting the organ to the church proved just as difficult. The local roads of the day were either impassable or non-existent. One of the men of the congregation carried the organ through the woods from a distant railway line, a truly Herculean feat.

By the later twentieth century the little log church had grown old, and needed repairs. Some of the logs had rotted. Unlike many other such buildings, Sand Lake Pioneer Church has had loving people who have taken a great interest in its preservation. The Ontario Ministry of Natural Resources, which supervises a stand of original pine nearby, gave the congregation permission to cut enough logs for restoration purposes. After the repairs were finished, it was difficult to tell the new logs from the old.

During the 1980s, the congregation decided to add a small belfry over the entranceway. A farm bell, which had carried messages to men in the fields for several generations, was donated. The bell was restored and installed in a belfry made from local, weathered barn boards.

Because of increasing numbers of cottagers and tourists during the summer months, Thursday evening services were organized. Soon the eighty-seat church was overflowing. A public address system was installed so that others could enjoy the service outside on the lawn. In mid-August, the casual visitor will be surprised to see that Christmas lights and decorations adorn Sand Lake Church and Christmas carols waft from the throats of the assembled. A summer Christmas service is now an annual event.

The place remains an inspiration to all who come. The flowers around the building are carefully tended by the parishioners, and the cemetery is lovingly cared for. An infant son of the family who originally donated the land for the church lies in an unmarked grave — the first burial in the cemetery. During the winter months the snow piles up on the pathway to the church door. Only the calls of northern jays break the silence, replacing the melodious voices that in summer still sing about "The Little Brown Church in the Vale."

34. Madill Church (United), 1873
Madill Church Road, south of Huntsville, Muskoka Region

*A*nother log church still survives on the near-northern frontier of Old Ontario that now serves as a prominent part of the province's cottage country. The building stands as a reminder of the many log churches which once dotted the more southerly landscape of early Upper Canada, but were subsequently replaced by more elaborate structures.

The Madill Church, just south of present-day Huntsville on Madill Church Road, is located in the increasingly expensive playground of the Muskoka Region, somewhat south of Sand Lake in Parry Sound. Government colonization roads in the 1850s and

Madill Church, near Huntsville.

1860s, and railways in the 1870s and 1880s, helped open the area up to new settlement (and the lumbering industry). Here, as in areas still further north, climate and geography finally conspired against any exact replication of the family farm frontier in the south. As in the case of Sand Lake, the Madill building managed to survive long enough to attract the attention of latter-day preservationists.

Built by Wesleyan Methodists, the Madill Church was constructed of squared timbers on land donated by John Madill, in 1873. Each family in the pioneer congregation contributed two logs and assisted in the construction. Including the base, ten logs form each wall. Unlike the Sand Lake Church logs, which were carefully broad-axed to produce a smooth surface, the Madill Church logs were roughly finished. Their protruding knots still give an interesting appearance. Arched Gothic windows, unusual in this type of building, also give the Madill Church a jaunty, confident facade.

Designated as an official historic site by the Ontario government, the church has been kept in good repair through the efforts of many local people. John Madill's daughter, Mrs. Edward Armstrong, paid to redecorate the building in 1935. The dry-stone foundation was rebuilt in 1968 by Les Helstern and Wilson Cairns. The Madill Church plays host to numerous weddings today, and the United Church of Canada conducts a memorial service in July each year, to honour the early pioneers of the present-day Muskoka Region.

Lennox & Addington County

35.Church of St. Alban the Martyr (Anglican), 1884
10419 Highway 33, Adolphustown, Town of Greater Napanee

*Thou in thy mercy hast led forth the people which
thou hast redeemed: thou has guided them in
thy strength unto thy holy habitation.*
Exodus 15:13

*B*y the later nineteenth century Old Ontario itself had begun to look back at some of the earlier pioneering experiences in the southern part of the province.

On June 16, 1784, United Empire Loyalists from the new American republic had landed at Adolphustown, in what is now the Town of Greater Napanee, in Lennox & Addington County. One hundred years later, in the summer of 1884, Adolphustown was one of three Ontario communities that held special celebrations to commemorate "The Centennial of the Settlement of Upper Canada by the United Empire Loyalists." (The Adolphustown celebrations were held in June. Parallel events took place in Toronto in July, and in Niagara in August. It is said that the York Pioneers in Toronto had been plotting such schemes since 1876, when the Americans across the lake had celebrated the centennial of the Declaration of Independence.)

Possibly the oldest church bell in Canada.

Not altogether by accident, the Loyalist centennial of 1884 also marks the completion of St. Alban the Martyr Anglican Church in Adolphustown, which still stands today. It was named after an early martyr of Britain in the days of the Roman empire. A citizen of Verulam (in present-day Hertford-shire), Alban hid an early Christian priest from Roman persecution.

Converted to Christianity by the priest, St. Alban was subsequently tortured and executed himself. According to legend, he performed several miracles on the way to his beheading.

Many, many years later, in the days of Britain's own empire, some similar miracle brought the Reverend Forneri to the new Canadian province of Ontario. A political refugee from a new kind of late nineteenth-century Italy, Forneri became fascinated with United Empire Loyalism. When it was suggested that suitable memorials be erected at Adolphustown to honour the Loyalist centennial in 1884, he immediately thought of a church. Forneri and a local committee chose a scaled-down design said to be based on Montréal's Anglican Christ Church Cathedral.

Church of St. Alban the Martyr, Adolphustown.

This was certainly not the first Anglican place of worship in Adolphustown. Reverend John Langdon had begun the ministry of the Church of England in the area in the 1780s, and a wood frame church built in 1822 still stands just west of the St. Alban the Martyr. As one drives around a bend on the Loyalist Parkway today, however (also known as Highway 33), it is the little limestone church of 1884, sitting in solitary splendour by the roadside, that catches the eye. Years ago, the round bell tower, now reconstructed, blew down during a severe storm. The bell, made in Bristol, England, in 1690, and now housed in a small tower at the front of the church, is believed to be the oldest church bell in Canada.

Another unusual feature of the church is sixty-two ceramic plaques, bordering the walls under the stained-glass windows. Donated by their descendants of the 1880s, the plaques list the names of Loyalists and other pioneers who settled in the area a century before. (Visitors with U.E.L. ancestors may find some of their the names on the lists.)

The Adolphustown area is still quite steeped in Loyalist sentiment, even today. Two replicas of the regimental colours carried by Rogers Rangers, who fought on the British side in the American Revolution, were hung in the Church of St. Alban the Martyr in 1984 — to celebrate the bicentennial of "the Settlement of Upper Canada by the United Empire Loyalists" in June 1784. Though the church is now closed except for weddings and funerals, a special memorial service is still held each year to honour the coming of the Loyalists. Many people in the area were especially pleased when, with support from all three major political parties, the Ontario legislature voted to declare June 19 United Empire Loyalists' Day in the province, in 1997.

Leeds County

36. St. Brendan's Roman Catholic Church, 1891
Rockport, Thousand Islands, Front of Escott

*Upon this rock I will build my church; and the
gates of Hell will not prevail against it.*
Matthew 16:18

Though Anglicanism is sometimes characterized as an Anglo-Catholic rather than a
strictly Protestant faith, Reverend Forneri had strayed at least somewhat from the
Roman Catholicism of his original native land when he helped create an Anglican church
in Adolphustown. But as a matter of public policy, the mixed community of Oliver
Mowat's Ontario was still receptive to Roman Catholics (who had, among other things,
enjoyed some representation among the Loyalists themselves). An example here is St.
Brendan's Roman Catholic Church near present-day Rockport in Leeds County, another
county again to the east of Lennox and Addington.

St. Brendan's was erected on an unusually firm foundation in 1891. Today it remains
a picturesque white wood-frame church on the banks of the St. Lawrence River, set on
a chunk of very solid primeval granite from the Canadian Shield. It is said that the building was constructed by thirteen families of Irish origin who had found their way to the
Thousand Islands in Ontario. They hauled sand and gravel from nearby areas and
dragged locally hewn lumber over the rocks to the site. Wooden ladders were used to
carry bundles of shingles onto the steeply sloped roof. The stained-glass windows were
transported by rowboat down the river from Kingston.

On its rocky bluff overlooking the water, the church was positioned in such a way
that the priest, while officiating at mass, could watch the boats on the river. The steeple,
surmounted by a cross, still provides a landmark for the traffic on the St. Lawrence.
Every Sunday morning travellers on the river can hear the bell, high in the belfry,
resounding over the waters. Many of the early parishioners lived on the nearby islands
and, in winter, made their way across the frozen river to attend mass.

The church is named after the Irish patron saint of sailors, navigators, and explorers.

Born circa 486 in the Vale of Tralee, County Kerry, Ireland, St. Brendan was educated in a monastery and became a missionary priest. One suspects that he was an adventurer at heart, however, for he made many voyages, mapping the Hebrides and parts of southern Europe. He explored the islands of the North Sea, including the Shetlands and Faroes, and he is credited with the discovery of the Canary Islands. He is also believed to have brought Christianity to the Picts, the fierce early peoples of Scotland who kept the Roman legions at bay.

According to a particular Irish legend, St. Brendan was the first European discoverer of the New World as well. Clouded in controversy, the legend would have us believe that fifteen hundred years ago — four hundred years ahead of Leif Ericson, and almost a thousand years before Columbus — St. Brendan and his brawny crew sailed across the Atlantic

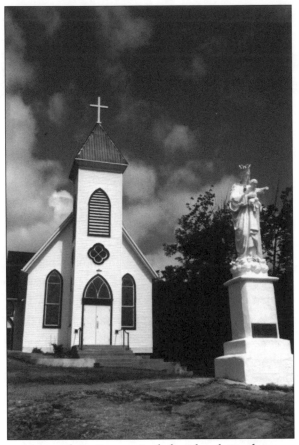

St. Brendan's Roman Catholic Church, Rockport.

from Ireland in a so-called curragh. This was a boat made from hides stretched across a wooden framework, to create a waterproof craft. (A similar type of vessel, made from canvas rather than hides, is apparently still used by Irish fishermen.) The round trip, from Ireland to the New World and back, is said to have lasted seven years.

As it happens, the story of a bearded giant who piloted a boat of skins would be recounted to other Europeans, centuries later, by aboriginal peoples in the West Indies. Was this St. Brendan and his fearless crew? In the 1970s, a group of present-day adventurers decided to test the feasibility of the legend. They duplicated the reputed voyage of St. Brendan and his sturdy sailors by crossing the Atlantic in a replica of the ancient curragh, carefully crafted from tanned cowhides. After a perilous six-week sail they arrived safely in Newfoundland, demonstrating, at least, that the Irish patron saint of seafarers *could* have made the 3500-mile journey across the sea.

In front of St. Brendan's Roman Catholic Church near Rockport, Ontario, today, standing on a protruding rock and cradling the infant Jesus in her arms, is a beautiful statue of Mary, Queen of Peace. Like a guardian angel, she is an inspiration to all the river traffic. Modern lights have been installed at the base of the pedestal to serve as a beacon for sailors who pass by, on the present-day St. Lawrence Seaway.

Rockport itself, in the heart of the Thousand Islands where the Canadian Shield reaches down to the St. Lawrence River, is well-named. There is barely enough top soil on the Archaean (or very ancient) rock of the Shield for the growth of pines and other hardy coniferous trees. As with similar terrain in other parts of Ontario, the earlier pioneer farming community that reached its golden age in the nineteenth century has nowadays largely given way to the tourism industry (and some accompanying boat building). St. Brendan's Roman Catholic Church, on solid rock high above the St. Lawrence, is still watching over the present-day seafarers who make their way along what French Canadians once called the River of Canada.

City of Toronto

37. Holy Blossom Temple (Reform Jewish), 1897 (1938)
1950 Bathurst Street, south of Eglinton

He hath shewed thee, O man, what is good
and what doth the Lord require of thee,
but to do justly, and to love mercy,
and to walk humbly with thy God?
Micah 6:8

By the late nineteenth century Oliver Mowat's mixed community in Ontario had begun to show some deeper signs of its continuing expansion in the new century that lay ahead. In September 1897, the dedication of Holy Blossom Temple on Bond Street, in the province's rapidly growing capital city of Toronto, reflected both progress in a growing local Jewish community, and the early stages in the development of an increasingly more diverse provincial society.

At this point small numbers of Jews from Great Britain and a few other parts of western Europe had been in the city for a few generations. Toronto's first synagogue owed something in particular to the arrival of Lewis Samuel in the 1850s. Born in Hull, England, Lewis had earlier moved with his parents to Syracuse, New York, where he married Kate Seckleman. After the birth of their children, the young couple had moved to Montréal. From here they moved to Toronto, in July 1855. They took the new Grand Trunk Railway from Montréal to Prescott, Canada West, where they had to board a boat for the remainder of the journey.

When the Samuels arrived in Toronto, there were only about thirty-five Jewish families living in the city, some of whom had come as early as 1817. While a house of worship was always important to newly arrived immigrants, a burial ground often had to precede a sanctuary.

An 1828 act of the old Upper Canadian legislature had given all religious denominations in the province the right to hold land in perpetuity for purposes of burial grounds. In 1849, the trustees of a newly formed "Hebrew Congregation of the City of Toronto" purchased land on present-day Pape Avenue for the first Jewish cemetery on Ontario soil. One of the earliest tombstones marks the death of Charlotte Nordheimer at the tender age of nine years.

In 1856, the recently arrived Lewis Samuel urged that the modest but steadily growing Toronto Jewish community also needed a synagogue of its own. A group known as the "Toronto Hebrew Congregation (Sons of Israel)" began to hold services at rented premises over Coombe's drugstore, at the corner of Richmond and Yonge streets. This group soon joined with the earlier group that had started the cemetery. By 1871 the resulting Toronto Hebrew Congregation had officially adopted the name Holy Blossom. By the middle of the 1870s the rented premises over Coombe's drugstore had become inadequate for a community that continued to grow quietly. A building committee headed by Lewis Samuel bought land on the south side of Richmond Street, just east of Victoria. Here the first synagogue built in Ontario was officially opened in January 1876. Popularly known as the Richmond Street synagogue, it was the ancestor of both subsequent Holy Blossom Temples.

Traditionally, Jewish men and women worshipped separately. In the Richmond Street synagogue the women sat in the balcony and the men downstairs. To further separate the sexes, some very orthodox members put up a curtain so the men could not see the women. When the ladies staged an open revolt, the curtain was taken down. A small wind of change was beginning to blow through what was still a traditional congregation.

In 1890, the board of the Richmond Street synagogue had agreed to the use of an organ for the forthcoming festival of Passover. The more orthodox brethren felt that any musical instrument in the synagogue was a violation of the laws laid down in the Torah. Incensed by such effrontery, the cantor resigned and a tug of war ensued. Three members picked up the organ and carried it out into the yard. Other members, just as determined to have an organ, picked it up and carried it back inside.

The now long-demolished Richmond Street synagogue has been described as "not a very imposing structure." The new larger and more impressive Holy Blossom Temple dedicated in September 1897 was located on Bond Street, just north of the main Methodist and Roman Catholic churches in the downtown Toronto of the day. Unfortunately, Lewis Samuel did not live to see the fulfillment of this particular dream, but his son, Sigmund Samuel, would take on much of his father's earlier role in the congregation. The congregation itself was still torn between those who wanted to institute reforms that would help Judaism fit into the life of the modern world, and the orthodox members who believed that they must adhere to Judaism as it had been preserved since the time of Abraham. Another musical struggle arose over whether Holy Blossom should have a women's choir. (In the early days, there had not even been a men's choir: a cantor chanted the prayers and the congregation followed him in lowered voices.) Finally, in 1920, Holy Blossom officially affiliated with the Reform movement in the United States.

By the 1920s the life of the old British and west European Jewish community in Toronto had changed enormously from the days of Lewis Samuel. In the late nineteenth and early twentieth centuries the city was one of several Canadian destinations for large-scale Jewish migration from eastern Europe — an early part of the increasingly diverse Canadian mosaic that, with some interruptions, has continued to develop, down to the present. By the time of the 1931 census Jews would account for more than seven percent of Toronto's population, making up the fourth largest ethnic group in the city, after English, Irish, and Scottish. Many of the newcomers were poor and initially had little knowledge of English. The more established congregation at Holy Blossom Temple on Bond Street was called upon to assist them, often providing shelter, clothing, and food. As poor as they began, many descendants of the newcomers would become lawyers, doctors, and business people.

During the earlier twentieth century, many new synagogues arose to accommodate the city's burgeoning Jewish population. The more established Holy Blossom, however, continued to attract new members. By the late 1930s the time had come to move to still larger and more impressive quarters. On May 28, 1938, the present Holy Blossom Temple on Bathurst Street at Ava Road was dedicated. The now obsolete building on Bond Street would pass into the hands of Christian brethren and become the Greek Orthodox Church of St. George.

Today Holy Blossom in Toronto is the only synagogue to bear that name and some mystery has surrounded its origin. Possibly the first time the name appeared was in the minutes of an 1862 board meeting of the trustees. Young men who were being prepared for religious occupations were referred to as "Pirchay Kodesh" or "Holy Blossoms." According to some authorities, the "s" was dropped to become Holy Blossom Temple.

Whatever its origin, the name seems appropriate for the present architectural gem on Bathurst Street, so well harmonized with its surrounding landscape. Built from monolithic concrete in the Romanesque style, it takes the form of a basilica. Occupying one whole block, the front entrance is about six feet above street level. Guarding the main entrance are two stately lions, the traditional symbols of the tribe of Judah. Seven steps of Queenston limestone (suggesting the seven days of creation) lead to the three entrance doors, each divided into six panels. Hand-carved symbols in the panels are meant to convey the fundamental teachings of Judaism.

Defying the tradition of placing the altar so that the congregants face Jerusalem, the altar is located in the west end of the building. The Ark is reached by a flight of five steps symbolic of the Five Books of Moses. Suspended from a highly decorated grille, the Ner Tomid or Eternal Light casts a rosy glow above the Ark. Situated over the balconies in the sanctuary, a series of eight stained-glass windows depict the religious and historical

Holy Blossom Temple on Bathurst Street in Toronto.

development of Israel. A beautiful rose window on the facade of the sanctuary, donated in memory of his parents by Sigmund Samuel, is surrounded by twelve circular openings which portray the emblems of the twelve tribes of Judah. An eighty-two-foot memorial tower, giving a splendid view of the city, contains a continuous light that symbolizes the ancient fire that was to be kept burning in the Holy Temple in Jerusalem.

Founded by Abraham, Judaism has a tradition that reaches back to early recorded history. Although there are three distinct divisions in contemporary North American Jewry — Orthodox, Conservative, and Reform — they all adhere to the concept that there is only one God. It is from this concept that both Christianity and Islam were born. Scattered across the globe and vastly outnumbered among the world's population, the adherents of Judaism have managed to survive, in spite of relentless persecution. Jewish tradition accepts the Hebrew Bible as the disclosure of God's will and the early history of the Jewish people. It is one of the greatest and most influential literary works of the world.

The Jewish people of Canada have made their own significant contributions to the country. As early as the War of 1812–14, members of the Jewish community have served in the military. For five generations, members of what is said to be the first Jewish family to settle in Canada, the Harts, have participated in every war in which Canada has been engaged. Two of their sons were killed in the First World War.

Among the outstanding personalities who have been associated with the Holy Blossom Temple in Toronto are Senator David Croll, Ontario's first Jewish cabinet minister in the 1930s (who swore his oath of office on the Torah); Nathan Phillips, the first Jewish mayor of Toronto in the 1950s; Bora Laskin, chief justice of Canada in the 1970s and early 1980s; Rose Wolfe, chancellor of the University of Toronto; Sigmund Samuel, the philanthropist who donated both his art collection and the Canadiana building in which to house it; and Rabbi Gunther Plaut, who was awarded the Order of Canada for his work in the field of human rights. These and other members of the congregation have worked hard to promote a province and a country where all citizens can enjoy freedom on an equal basis. Besides its own unique Jewish leadership, Holy Blossom has helped create a wiser, more understanding mixed community in Ontario today.

The Twentieth Century

*A*n already aging Oliver Mowat had resigned as premier of Ontario in 1896, to join the new Liberal federal government of Canada's first French Canadian prime minister, Sir Wilfrid Laurier. But Mowat's old Liberal provincial government lived on under less gifted leadership until 1905, when the provincial Conservatives under James Pliny Whitney finally took charge.

The early twentieth century marked a turning point for the province in other ways as well. The federal census of 1911, for the first time in its still short history, showed almost equal numbers of urban and rural residents Ontario-wide. It testified to a long decline in the golden age of the family farm that would not improve over the next half-century. The half-dozen largest urban areas in the province of the day were Toronto (with a population of some 478,000 people), Ottawa (133,000), Hamilton (112,000), present-day Kitchener-Waterloo (63,000), London (61,000), and Windsor (32,000).

In 1912 Ontario officially assumed its present boundaries — from the Ottawa River to the Lake of the Woods, and from the Great Lakes all the way north to Hudson Bay. The province played various roles in the growth of western Canada. But northern or, as was often said at the time, "New" Ontario was its own new frontier. High hopes for a second round of agricultural settlement on the so-called northern Clay Belt would be disappointed. Northern Ontario nonetheless opened up vast new opportunities for the lumbering and pulp and paper industries. Mining on the Canadian Shield in the north would stimulate the growth of the Toronto financial district, and soften the local blows of the Great Depression in the 1930s.

Meanwhile, especially the more central and westerly parts of southern Ontario had acquired a modern industrial base. Hamilton had a new steel industry. "Branch plants" in such places as Windsor and Oshawa started to manufacture American automobiles, for both the Canadian domestic market and the wider markets of the British empire. On its own home ground, Ontario would remain a place unusually well served by railways until the middle of the twentieth century. By the end of the First World War, however, the ultimately triumphant age of the automobile had settled in. The often very rugged roads of the nineteenth century had begun to improve noticeably by the 1920s. By the 1950s the construction of the province's present contribution to the automobile-friendly highway system of North America was well underway.

The two world wars themselves (1914–1918 and 1939–1945) were important local events. In both cases Canada, unlike the neighbouring United States (but like Great Britain), was in at the beginning. Hundreds of thousands of young men from Ontario volunteered to defend freedom overseas. The young women who took over the jobs they left behind set precedents with loud echoes in the later twentieth century. In Ontario, as in other places, the successive miracles of indoor plumbing, central heating, electrical household appliances, the telephone, radio, movies, air travel, and television would transform everyday life as the century progressed.

There were especially vigorous waves of new arrivals to the province during the decades just before the First and just after the Second World War. Initially, immigrants from Great Britain were still in the majority. But new pioneers from an increasingly greater variety of other places were more numerous, especially after the Second World War.

Wherever they came from, at least most of the new arrivals of the twentieth century would settle in rising cities, suburbs, and towns, not on old family farms. By the census of 1961 more than three-quarters of the Ontario population was living in urban areas. The Toronto metropolitan region alone was home to almost two million people. Ottawa had almost half a million, Hamilton some 359,000, Windsor 192,000, London 181,000, and Kitchener-Waterloo 177,000. The total population of Ontario had grown from about two-and-a-half million people in 1911 to some six-and-a-quarter million in 1961. The province that would celebrate the Canadian centennial of 1967 was a quite different kind of place than it had been a century before.

According to the publisher of the *Telegram* in Toronto, John Ross Robertson (1841–1918), Ontario's capital city in the earlier twentieth-century had been a "city of churches." By the early 1960s sentiments of this sort were losing their resonance among younger people. But the new United Church of Canada that was established in 1925 had reflected new kinds of thinking about both the future of Christianity and the future of Canada. Ontario's first Jewish cabinet minister, David Croll, swore his oath of office on the Torah in 1935. Especially after the Second World War, increasing numbers of new arrivals from the Catholic countries of Europe were making the Roman Catholic Church in the province more important than it had been in the nineteenth century. By the early 1960s a few new arrivals had begun to bring a still more diverse variety of deeply felt religious commitments to a changing Ontario society. In some old and some new ways, the life of the spirit carried on.

City of Toronto

38. St. Anne's Anglican Church, 1908
270 Gladstone Avenue, Dufferin & Dundas

O worship the Lord in the beauty of holiness.
Text below the organ pipes in St. Anne's.

*I*n May 1920 what is now the Art Gallery of Ontario, in Toronto, would hold an exhibition of "Paintings by a Group of Seven Canadian Artists" — introducing a fresh and more authentic way of looking at the rugged northern geography that the province still shares with other parts of the country. Some of the same artists would go on to decorate the sanctuary of the fifteen-year-old St. Anne's Anglican Church in the city's west end, and leave a legacy that still endures today.

Annexations of adjacent municipalities were important in Toronto's early twentieth-century growth. St. Anne's Anglican Church —whose traditional parish ran from present-day Dufferin Street west to the Humber River, and from Lake Ontario north to Davenport Road — was located in what had once been the sparsely populated village of Brockton. In its nineteenth-century youth Brockton had centred around a post office, a toll-gate, and three taverns. Then, among other things, the chocolate factory of the William H. Neilson Company (which had its own herd of dairy cattle) helped attract new settlers to the area.

When the population of the village had increased sufficiently, the adherents of the Church of England, who had to travel downtown to St. James Cathedral on King Street to attend services, deemed the time had come to build their own place of worship. The first organizational meeting was held over a pint of ale in The Brown Bear Tavern. A well-connected Roman Catholic family donated an acre of land, in honour of their Anglican mother. The original brick, Gothic-style St. Anne's was designed by the well-known architect Kivas Tully. Additions were added over the years until the church could seat seven hundred. This included seating for waifs from a nearby orphanage, whose religious training was considered to be of the utmost importance.

With the City of Toronto annexations of the early twentieth century, the need for a

St Anne's Anglican Church, Toronto.

larger structure became evident. In 1907, under the inspiration of a gifted new rector, the Reverend Lawrence Skey, the foundation stone of the present building was laid. (The building itself would not be completed until 1908). Modelled by the Toronto architect Ford Howland on the floor plan and dome of St. Sophia's in Istanbul, a pure Byzantine design was chosen. The basic concept of Byzantine architecture is a dome situated in the centre of the intersection of a Greek cross. As in many denominations, some local rivalry was reflected in the final plans. It is said that Reverend Skey wanted the new church in the new west end of Toronto to surpass St. James Cathedral downtown. Widening the arms of the cross in St. Anne's and opening up the transepts would realize part of the dream: the resulting new building would seat sixteen hundred people — two hundred more than St. James.

Some fifteen years after the church first opened, Reverend Skey seems to have decided that he was finally not satisfied with outdoing the Cathedral in mere seating capacity. He also wanted to turn the dull brownish interior of the still quite new St. Anne's into a beautiful monument. Under the direction of his friend, J.E.H. MacDonald, nine painters and two sculptors created some impressive works of art on the dome, ceilings, and walls of the church. Disregarding the Gothic canopied stained-glass windows, they decided on a flat Byzantine treatment combined with the illustrative style of later artists. Gold, crimson, Venetian red, yellow ochre, ultramarine blue, umber, permanent green, and ivory-white were used to brighten the walls.

Today one can still follow the main events in the life of Christ by starting with *The*

Nativity and proceeding through the chancel paintings to *The Ascension*. In defiance of the chronology of the Gospels, *The Transfiguration* has been placed in the central position above the altar.

J.E.H. MacDonald is usually said to have been the founder of the Group of Seven, and his work aroused great controversy among local art critics of the day. He painted *The Crucifixion* in St. Anne's — one of four pendentive paintings which are fifteen feet wide and ten feet high. He also painted *The Transfiguration* above the altar. Franklin Carmichael, a more elusive member of the Group, was responsible for two of the Apse paintings: *The Adoration of the Magi* and *Entry into Jerusalem*. Another Group member, F. H. Varley, did the dome paintings of Moses, Isaiah, Jeremiah, and Daniel. (Varley, who projected intense emotionalism into his work, saw green as a very spiritual colour, and used various shades of it in his art.)

Artists who were not part of the Group of Seven worked on St. Anne's Anglican Church in west Toronto as well. Frances Loring and Florence Wyle sculpted the four octagonal pieces of plaster moulding in high relief that represent the symbols of the evangelists (the eagle of St. John, the lion of St. Mark, the angel of St. Matthew, and the ox of St. Luke). The other painters were H.S. Palmer (*The Resurrection*), H.S. Stanfield (*The Ascension*), Arthur Martin (*Jesus in the Temple*), Neil Mackechnie (*The Palsied Man)*, Stewart Treviranus (*The Temptation* and *The Betrayal*), and Thoreau MacDonald (J.E.H. MacDonald's son, who did *The Raising of Lazarus*).

One can understand why the portrait of Judas was replaced by that of St. Matthias, but why was the portrait of St. James replaced by that of St. Paul? Did continuing rivalry between St. Anne's in the west end and St. James downtown reach such a peak that the Reverend Skey demanded the change of portraits so that the name of St. James would not appear in St. Anne's?

The real truth may never be known. The important point now is that even the present congregation of St. Anne's Anglican Church on Gladstone Avenue must sometimes pause and give thanks for a sanctuary of such magnificent art and great beauty in which to worship.

District of Thunder Bay

39. St. Peter's Church (Roman Catholic), 1911
615 Connolly Street, Thunder Bay

*And I have said, I will bring you up ... unto a
land flowing with milk and honey.*
Exodus 3:17

In the early twentieth century, new arrivals from various parts of central and eastern Europe found their way to northern or New Ontario, as well as to the cities of the south. St. Peter's Roman Catholic Church in present-day Thunder Bay, completed in 1911, is now the oldest surviving Slovak church in Canada and the second oldest in North America.

The altar of St. Peter's Church.

Joseph Bellon, who established a wireworks factory in Toronto in the 1870s, was among the first Slovaks to arrive in Canada. But the first real wave of Slovak immigrants did not materialize until the late nineteenth and early twentieth centuries. No fast jet transported them to their new land. The pioneers of the day still came by ship. Unlike Joseph Bellon, most had scant resources, and had to travel in steerage. The main things of value they brought with them were their Christian faith, their work ethics, their strong moral values, and a commitment to their new nation. They firmly believed that they were coming to a land of opportunity.

Although the federal government in Ottawa encouraged new Slovak immigrants to settle in western Canada, many eventually came to Ontario instead. Some settled in the north, around Fort William and Port Arthur on Lake Superior (now amalgamated into the City of Thunder Bay). They worked long hours in the mining and forestry industries. One pocket of settlement in Fort William developed along what was then called the Town Plot. Another in the area, beginning along the Kaministiqua River across from Mission Island, was on the original site of the old fur trading forts of the North West and Hudson's Bay companies. Near the water, the Canadian Pacific Railway had built a roadhouse and large coal maintenance facilities. Because of the job opportunities, Slovaks, Italians, and Ukrainians flocked to the "Coal Docks." For ten cents an hour they toiled ten to twelve hours a day.

Apart from hard work, the life of the Slovak newcomers revolved

St Peter's Roman Catholic Church, Thunder Bay.

around their families and their church. With the men outside the home for such long hours, the women became heads of households, and often took in boarders to augment the family income. The boarders would be favoured with sour soups, dumplings, sauerkraut, and other such dishes from the homeland.

Determined to have a place to worship, the members of the Catholic Slovak community in Fort William pledged sums of money from their hard-earned wages to build a church. In November 1907, just days before the new church was to be blessed, a fire raged through the building and completely destroyed it. Because the insurance only covered the builder's costs, the congregation had to dig deep once again, to raise enough money for a new structure. But in October 1911 the new brick building that still stands today was completed. A tower, enhanced by a domed cupola surmounted by a cross, provides the main entrance.

In 1931 an elaborate main altar replaced the old one of 1911. Originally designed for a church in North Bay, someone had miscalculated the size and found that it didn't fit. A side altar, incorporating the Last Supper tableau, has subsequently been built by members of the parish. The Stations of the Cross date back to the earliest days of the church and have descriptions written in the Slovak language. Adorning the ceiling are a series of paintings depicting the Holy Family and the saints, as well as Biblical scenes. These are the unique work of L. Scott Young, a Bay Street financier in Toronto who had an avocation for religious painting.

In Thunder Bay, as in other parts of the province, a great deal has changed since the arrival of the first Slovak immigrants in the early twentieth century. But St. Peter's on Connolly Street remains a vibrant parish that continues to fulfill the needs of the local community and all who continue to see it as their church home.

Waterloo Region

40. St. Jacobs Mennonite Church, 1916
St. Jacobs, north of Waterloo

> *Our future here in Canada very definitely lies*
> *in the land and not in the city, in the final*
> *analysis, on new land, our only prospect*
> *for settling in closed communities.*
> Jacob H. Jenzen (1878–1950)

The old rural southern Ontario has gone through various stages of decline and redevelopment in the twentieth century. But it has also continued to have its attractions. Even in the twenty-first century you can still hear the clip-clop of a horse's hooves ringing on the solid wooden planking as a buggy emerges from Ontario's only remaining covered bridge. Wide enough for one lane of horse-drawn vehicles or a modern car, the bridge at West Montrose is a reminder of bygone days. Built in 1881, six miles east of Elmira, in the present-day Waterloo Region, it has been dubbed the Kissing Bridge. The passenger in the buggy is probably a Mennonite woman, wearing a bonnet and clothing much like what pioneer women wore two centuries ago.

St. Jacobs Mennonite Church, which was built in nearby St. Jacobs in 1916, during the First World War, is still in use today. Originally Anabaptists, a religious group that broke away from the Catholic Church in sixteenth-century Europe, the first Mennonites considered themselves to be neither Catholic nor Protestant. Michael Sattler, a former priest, drafted a confession of Faith to which the most ardent believers still cling. Adherents practise baptism of mature, voluntary believers, celebrate the Lord's Supper not as a sacrament but in remembrance of Christ's suffering and death, abjure from the swearing of oaths, and adopt a policy of pacifism in the face of violence. Menno Simons, another former priest, assumed leadership of the movement in 1536: it is after him that the present-day Mennonite denomination is named.

The early Mennonites in Switzerland, the German states, and the Netherlands were often persecuted for their beliefs. Substantial numbers had moved to Pennsylvania in the British American colonies by the end of the seventeenth century. Strong attachments to the spiritual virtues of agrarian life had also helped push them to the New World, where land was available. During the American Revolution, their pacifism had made them unpopular with many of their more patriotic neighbours. New land for settlement in Upper Canada was an added attraction for growing families. German-speaking Mennonites from Pennsylvania were among those who moved north of the Great Lakes after the War of Independence.

They came on foot and on horseback, and some arrived in Conestoga wagons drawn by four- and six-horse teams. The journey was often complicated by hazards. The Conestoga wagons decreased the danger as their wide wheels resisted sinking into the soft, muddy road beds. With their billowing white canvass covers, they protected precious cargo from soaking rains and blistering sun. The women and children often walked for miles as the loads were too heavy and the roads too muddy to carry passengers. Sometimes the wagons upset in the mud. One campground witnessed the loss of three horses when a huge tree fell on them.

German-speaking Mennonite migrants from Pennsylvania settled in several parts of Upper Canada. By the early nineteenth century a substantial group had put down roots along the Grand River in the present-day Waterloo Region. Here they became the nucleus for a larger community that would also attract German-speaking immigrants from Europe. The community was focussed around a settlement first known as Ebytown, and then officially renamed Berlin. In the midst of local controversy during the First World War, Berlin, Ontario, was renamed Kitchener after a general of the British empire.

The old Mennonite preachers and teachers were chosen by lot from among the congregation. A slip of paper with the text of Proverbs 16:33 written on it ("The lot is cast into the lap; but the whole disposing thereof is of the Lord") was inserted into a Bible or hymn book and then placed among a number of others. Whether the best candidate or not, the one who drew the book with the slip became the preacher or teacher.

As elsewhere in Upper Canada, building agricultural settlements along the Grand River had been a struggle. Many of the implements were handmade from wood. First harvests were cut with a sickle or scythe. Grain threshing, done by flail, took all winter. A forest fire raged through the community in 1806, destroying houses, barns, fences, and animals. In 1816 frost covered the ground every single month of the year. In June the ice was thick enough to bear the weight of a horse-drawn wagon on a pond. Heavy snow fell as late as June 26. Food for both people and animals was scarce the following winter.

Legislated exemptions from compulsory military service had been one of the special attractions of Upper Canada for Mennonites in the late eighteenth and early nineteenth centuries. The conscription that was finally imposed by the Dominion of Canada during the First World War changed things. Dissatisfied with this and other conditions of life in

Ontario in the early twentieth century (when the present Mennonite church in St. Jacobs was erected), some members of the community moved to Mexico in the 1920s. They found that life in Mexico offered even less freedom than in Canada, however, and there was a significant return to the Kitchener area. During the Second World War, Canada granted Mennonites the status of conscientious objectors if they wished to be exempted from military service.

Another wave of Mennonites from Europe would arrive in Ontario after the Second World War. Better educated and more liberal in their thinking, they began to place more stress on financial considerations than religious and cultural concerns. Many were professional people and chose to be urban dwellers. Less than a quarter of the estimated 50,000 Mennonites who live in Ontario today are still on farms (and there is even a Chinese Mennonite Church in Toronto). Yet though the community has, like everyone else in the province at large, shifted from a predominantly agrarian society to a more urban one, a core group around St. Jacobs and Elmira in Waterloo Region continues to cling to the old rural lifestyle.

Here Old Order Mennonites still arrive at their meeting houses by horse and buggy. Meeting houses, like the one in nearby Elmira, are often square, unpainted clapboard

St. Jacobs Mennonite Church.

buildings. No ornamentation disturbs the bare interior where men and women sit on opposite sides. For the most part the visual arts are rejected, but music making and choral singing have been highly developed. Old Order Mennonites are also especially skilled in such practical arts as furniture making. Anyone who has visited their markets has seen the intricate quilts the women have made. Although carving and sculpture are frowned upon, doll making is permissible. In 1982, one of Helga Broun's Mennonite dolls adorned one of Canada's postage stamps.

A people highly skilled in agricultural pursuits, the Old Order Mennonites' love of the land makes them ideal guardians of rural areas in an age of quite different new obsessions. Determined to preserve their peaceful and uncluttered way of life, and rejecting all artifices of a more worldly society, they are nonetheless always ready to extend a helping hand when their more worldly fellow human beings are in trouble. After the terrible ice storm disaster of 1998, they arrived in eastern Ontario with their traditional equipment and expertise to aid the victims. Today the Mennonites who still cling to the old ways are living examples of Ontario's earlier pioneer heritage. Driving through their country in the Waterloo Region is a trip back in time — and another very interesting facet of the province's current multicultural society.

District of Nipissing

41. L'Église Sacré-Coeur de Jésus, 1918
Corbeil, southeast of North Bay

Suffer the little children to come unto me, and forbid
them not: for of such is the kingdom of God.
Mark 10:14

As the First World War was ending, in 1918, work had begun on the second incarnation of l'Église Sacré-Coeur de Jésus in the small community of Corbeil, Ontario, just east of Lake Nipissing, along the old fur trade canoe corridor that followed the Ottawa, Mattawa, and French rivers to Georgian Bay (and where, some still say, northern Ontario really begins).

In the later nineteenth century French Canadians from Québec had begun to move west into this and other parts of Ontario — returning to the particular pioneering work that Brûlé and Champlain and Father Le Caron had started, some 275 years before. The province of the earlier twentieth century would be somewhat less receptive to the trend than Oliver Mowat's mixed community had been. But today just under five percent of Ontario's population reports French as a mother tongue, more than ten percent claims some form or degree of single or mixed French ethnic origins, and twelve percent claims an ability to speak French (which is now quite clearly one of Canada's two official languages).

The arrival of the Canadian Pacific Railway in North Bay in 1882, just northwest of Corbeil, had helped open the area up to new settlement. Lumbering had replaced the fur trade by this point. As the lumbering industry grew, a small number of French Canadian families settled on the few pockets of land half-suitable for farming. By 1893 Corbeil had sufficient families to build its first very simple church. A quarter century later, the building had become inadequate and the families decided to build a larger structure. Just as the foundation was finished in 1918 the Spanish flu epidemic struck and all work ceased. A roof was built over the foundation and the congregation worshiped in the crypt or basement of the church for the next twenty-three years. (The building was finally completed and blessed by the bishop in 1941.)

In between the two world wars, while attending Mass in the crypt of the still-unfinished l'Église Sacré-Coeur de Jésus in Corbeil, sixteen-year-old Elzire Legros caught the eye of twenty-two-year-old Oliva Dionne. Soon they were married in the church. Oliva had the only car in the neighbourhood, except for the one owned by the priest. After the young couple honeymooned in the Ottawa Valley, they settled into the one-and-a-half-storey log house on Oliva's 195-acre farm, halfway between Corbeil and Callander. The area still had few amenities: no electricity, no telephone, no running water, and no local doctor. The life of the largely French Canadian community revolved around the family and the church.

In this still quite rugged northern environment, in the early morning hours of May 28, 1934, Elzire Dionne gave birth to what the outside world considered a miracle: five tiny females weighing a total of 13 pounds, 5 ounces. In the short period of her marriage she had produced a total of eleven children (one of whom died). The youngest was only eleven months old when "the quints" were born. Within the space of one year, Elzire had given birth to six children!

The quints also arrived in the midst of the Great Depression. The Canada-wide unemployment rate had skyrocketed to more than nineteen percent in 1933, and remained above fourteen percent in 1934 and 1935. Government social services were still rudimentary at best. Locally the situation was even worse. It is said that seventy percent of Callander's population was on public relief in the mid-1930s. Free meals were dispensed from the nearby North Bay jail. During the long winters, hundreds of transient men crowded into the jail each night to keep from freezing.

Although the Dionnes were better off than most of their neighbours (they were never on relief), the arrival of five extra children at once placed a severe financial burden on the young family. The government of Ontario, also concerned about various forms of private exploitation of the quints, placed them in a specially built hospital under the public care of Dr. Allan Roy Dafoe, who had arrived in time to deliver the last three of the five girls at their birth. For the larger community the advent of the quintuplets turned out to be a blessing. The outside world wanted to know about the miracle, and it was prepared to pay. Within two years there was no need for a relief office in Callander, which suddenly found itself on the main bus route to the large cities. Land values escalated and hotels flourished. Almost everyone seemed to cash in.

Things never did turn out so well, however, for the Dionne family and the quintuplets themselves. As young children the girls were separated from their parents and, as adults, the estrangement became complete: the Dionne Quintuplets moved to Québec on their eighteenth birthday. Two years later they would be together for the last time. Alone in her bed in a convent in St. Agathe, Emilie died during an epileptic seizure in August

A drawing of l'Église Sacré-Coeur de Jésus, Corbeil, before it burned down.

The Dionne Quintuplets Museum.

1954. In a lonely grove surrounded by the northern forest, her family gathered to bury her in the Corbeil cemetery. Separated from her parents in life, she would also be separated in death. Situated apart from the grave of her parents, a simple monument asking that she rest in peace marks her grave today.

Four years later, in a lavish wedding at l'Église Sacré-Coeur de Jésus in Corbeil, Cecile married Philippe Langlois. Tragedy would stalk their marriage. They were blessed with five children but one baby, a twin, died at the age of six months. Marie, who had secretly married Florian Houle, left behind two children when she died alone in February 1970. Today Yvonne, who never married, and Cecile and Annette, now divorced from their husbands, live together in a Montréal suburb. To compensate for their suffering and losses while on display to the world — and perhaps to atone for its own public role in exploiting the local miracle of the 1930s — the government of Ontario awarded the three survivors $4 million in March 1998.

The Dionne Quintuplets remain well known in the outside world. The house where they were born, now a museum, has been moved to a field on the outskirts of North Bay. Every year tourists wander through the rooms and gaze at the double bed where Elzire gave birth to the famous babies. The iron stove that kept them warm occupies a corner of the kitchen. Five identical dresses are on view, hanging in a row. Outside, on a grassy square, is an intriguing monument created by Peter Wolf Toth, and inscribed "Nipissing, the trail of the whispering giants." It reminds us of the area's first peoples and their heritage of the canoe and portage, which did so much to first bring the vastness of Canada to the world's attention.

L'Église Sacré-Coeur de Jésus in Corbeil has lived through its own ordeal. In June 1977 lightning struck the building that was begun in 1918. As Monseigneur Maurice Gaudreault and his parishioners stood helplessly by, the church burned to the ground. In the end the congregants were undaunted by the tragedy. Four years later, a new, modern structure crowned the knoll where the Dionne family attended Mass. In this latest incarnation the church where Elzire Legros first caught the eye of Oliva Dionne — and where the story of the Dionne Quintuplets ultimately began — still lives on, surrounded by the forest.

Ottawa-Carleton Region

42. St. Matthew's Anglican Church, 1929
217 First Avenue, Ottawa

And now unto Him, who is able to do all things
wisely and well for our good, be all the praise
and the glory, now and forever.
Favourite benediction of
Charles Hamilton (1834–1919)

The stock market crash of 1929 that led to the Great Depression of the 1930s came as a surprise to many different building projects in various parts of the world. An Ontario case in point is the present St. Matthew's Anglican Church in the Glebe neighbourhood of Ottawa — far to the south and east of Corbeil, along the historic Ottawa River canoe route.

The oldest Protestant church in Ottawa today is St. Andrew's Presbyterian on Kent Street, founded in 1828 in the new community then known as Bytown. This had been especially distressing to the great Anglican lion of Upper Canada, John Strachan, when he visited the place in the same year. Strachan was devoted to the concept that the Church of England should be the official religion of the province — and the sole beneficiary of the clergy reserves, or land set aside for "the support of a Protestant clergy" in the act of the British parliament that had created Upper Canada in 1791. Strachan was chagrined to find that the Presbyterians, Catholics, and Methodists had all founded churches in the Bytown area before the Anglicans. He was a man of considerable if not decisive influence, and his concerns brought results when the present Anglican Cathedral in Ottawa, Christ Church Cathedral on Sparks Street downtown, was established in 1832.

In the early nineteenth century Philemon Wright had begun to pioneer the lumbering industry in what is now Hull, Québec, on the opposite shore of the Ottawa River. Bytown itself was laid out by Lieutenant Colonel John By in 1827, as part of the work on the construction of the Rideau Canal. It rapidly eclipsed Wrightsville (later Hull), and developed into what a British writer would characterize as a "sub-Arctic lumbering village" of some importance. In 1855 it was incorporated as the City of Ottawa. Two years later, in response to a request from feuding Canadian legislators, Queen Victoria chose Ottawa as a capital for the old United Province of Canada. As she noted from a map, it was on the border between present-day Ontario and Québec. On a similar logic, it became the capital city of the new Dominion of Canada in 1867.

As Canada's capital city grew in the later nineteenth century, it expanded south onto what had originally been 178 acres of clergy reserves granted to St. Andrew's Presbyterian Church, as the first Protestant church in the immediate area. If John Strachan had prevailed as he wished back in old Upper Canada, Presbyterians would not have been granted clergy reserves at all. But his influence had never been quite that decisive. Part of the Ottawa area involved is still known as "the Glebe" today, after the English name for land granted in support of clergy. By the 1890s increasing numbers of Church of England adherents in the area had prompted the establishment of another Ottawa Anglican church. Its first service was held in January 1898, in a room above the grocery store of a C. Moreland. That evening a snowstorm swept across the city and brought the streetcars to a standstill. Although the young priest and his wife, undaunted by the weather, arrived in a covered sleigh, only thirteen parishioners braved the severe storm.

In the same year the son of a wealthy lumber family, Charles Hamilton, had become the first bishop of the Anglican diocese of Ottawa. A former rector of St. Matthew's in Québec City, he chose the same name for the new Anglican church in the Ottawa Glebe. With an irony that would no doubt have chagrined John Strachan even more, St. Matthew's followers purchased a 200-by-103-foot lot from St. Andrew's Presbyterian Church, and in the summer of 1898 a wood frame Anglican church was erected on the old Presbyterian glebe land. The building had clapboard siding, painted a light grey-blue with white trim around tall narrow windows. Said to be copied from the Guild Hall at the heart of the empire in London, the most impressive feature of the 260-seat structure was the hammer-beam trusses that supported the roof.

During the first few decades of the twentieth century, the Glebe area in Ottawa developed into a well-to-do residential community. St. Matthew's old wood-frame church found it increasingly difficult to cope with the needs of the parish, even though two transepts were added and the nave extended so that as many as seven hundred people could be seated in the building. At least the last half of the roaring 1920s had roared in Ontario. It seemed that the time was ripe for a larger and more imposing structure. Construction began in January 1929.

Led by Canon Jefferson, the congregation had enthusiastically campaigned for funds. Brought up in the Church of Ireland, Jefferson was a Low Churchman. He never wore vestments, and he did not want a cross over the altar, nor candles placed near the communion table. When he needed to ask his parishioners for money, he would never do it from the pulpit. Fund raising nonetheless became an obsession with the congregation. A large donation from a former mayor was matched by the parishioners. Hard-working women served meals from a booth at the Central Canada Exhibition. Bazaars were an eagerly awaited fund-raising event. Hopes for a new debt-free church ran high.

The grandest part of the dream was shattered by the stock market crash in October 1929. At this point the walls and roof of the new building were still unfinished. But the dedicated congregation decided to carry on, raising money by mortgaging several vacant lots that the parish owned. Construction continued and the first service in the new St. Matthew's was held in December of 1930.

Made from Indiana limestone, the building is in the

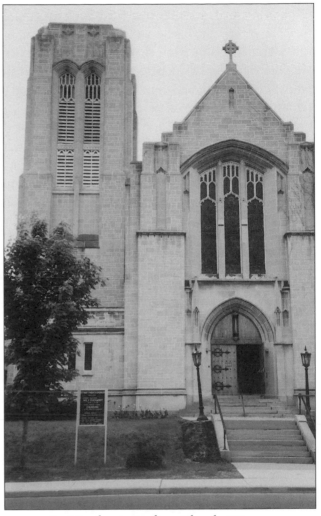

St. Matthew's Anglican Church, Ottawa.

orthodox cruciform style with a modified Gothic interior. British Columbia fir lends a solid foundation to the floors and hand-carved oak pews fill the nave. Stiff-backed pews from the old church supply the chapel. Artificial stone, stained with tea, gives the inside walls and arches the appearance of natural stone. A slate roof weighing 118 tons caps the structure. The squat tower at the north end accommodates eight bells. One can only wonder who designed the kitchen that some women of the church still refer to as Dante's Inferno.

St. Matthew's Anglican Church remains a vital force in the Glebe neighbourhood of

Ottawa today. It describes itself as "a Christ-centred, enthusiastic, and musical parish that has served the Glebe and Ottawa communities for a century." Along with several other churches in the older, more central parts of Ottawa, it operates a community support and counselling network. Its musical activities include one of the few surviving (and thriving) men and boys choirs left in Canada. The church organ is also one of Ottawa's largest, and some of its pipework dates back to the old building, where an organ made by the firm Casavant-Frères was installed in 1909. Enlarged by Casavant and installed in the new building in 1931, the organ was expanded again in 1957 by a firm from London, England. It is now in need of significant renovation and restoration. In May 2000 a special Vestry of the Parish voted overwhelmingly to go ahead with a new effort to raise the necessary funds, estimated at some $400,000.

City of Toronto

43. Calvary Baptist Church, 1929
72 Main Street, north of Kingston Road

We are the dead. Short days ago
We lived, felt dawn, saw sunset glow,
Loved and were loved, and now we lie
In Flanders' fields.

John McCrae (1872–1918)

There are some superficial chronological parallels between St. Matthew's Anglican Church in the Ottawa Glebe and Calvary Baptist Church in the east-end Beaches neighbourhood of Ontario's capital city. The present Calvary Baptist building in Toronto also dates back to the fateful year of 1929, and it similarly replaced an earlier building for a congregation that had been established in 1898. The present Calvary Baptist sanctuary, however, was added to the original structure of 1929 in 1953, with features that especially commemorate those who gave their lives in the Second World War. The result is that even in the old city of churches — full of many beautiful and outstanding houses of worship — Calvary Baptist is in a class of its own.

Coming from the most ardent spirit of the Reformation, by way of the old Anabaptists and English Puritans, Baptists today form the largest Protestant group in the United States (as opposed to the third-largest in Canada, and fourth-largest in Ontario). They believe that Christ is the Saviour of every true believer and that some form of life exists beyond death, and they are dedicated to a high degree of personal independence. Strong supporters of the individual's right to interpret the Bible, they have never adopted one of the historical Christian creeds. They believe in the supremacy of the Scriptures, in religious liberty and freedom, in the right to worship without interference from the state, and in the independence of the local church.

Baptists similarly do not have sacraments. The Lord's Supper, usually held on the first Sunday of the month, is simply observed in obedience to His command to commemorate His last supper on the night before He was crucified. Baptists are also notable for their rejection of infant baptism. They believe in the baptism of adult believers by full immersion, in the manner of John the Baptist at the River Jordan. Baptism in this sense is regarded as a public confession of Christian faith, and as a symbol of the burial and resurrection of Christ. New believers actually are baptized as adults. Young people raised in Baptist churches decide on their own if they wish to be baptized, often in their early adolescence.

Ministry is conceived by Baptists as a service to which all members of a local church are called. The role of the full-time pastor or minister is to preach, teach, counsel, train, and co-ordinate the ministries exercised by all members. Robert Sneyd, born in Port Hope, Ontario, had become the pastor at Calvary Baptist in east Toronto before the Second World War, in the new church building of 1929. All told, he would serve the church for forty-three years, retiring long after the war had ended. But his staunch faith and religious training as a Baptist preacher would stand him in particularly good stead for the six horrendous years that he ministered to the dead and dying, during the Second World War itself.

Major Sneyd had enlisted as a chaplain in the Canadian Army right at the start in 1939. In 1940 he went overseas to Europe, where he served his country until the end of the war in 1945. In September 1940, the day after the first bombing of London, he visited famed Westminster Abbey. He stood in front of a black marble slab that covered the final

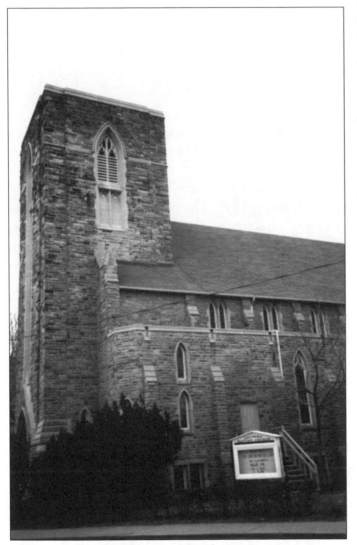

Calvary Baptist Church, Toronto.

resting place of an unknown soldier from the Great War of 1914–1918. High up in the clerestory, men were sweeping up the broken glass that had imploded during the bombing. Suddenly, several pieces clattered to the ground and came to rest on the marble tomb. When Major Sneyd stooped to pick up one insignificant fragment, an inspiration flashed through his mind. Hoping to return home someday, he decided to collect the stained glass shards from bombed churches wherever he was on duty. They would become a memorial window at Calvary Baptist in Toronto, to all those who gave their lives in the Second World War.

In Major Sneyd's book, *Broken Glass*, the reader is taken on a vivid journey through six years of war and destruction. Although he continued to collect his shards of glass, the dying and wounded were his first priority. Upon his return to Canada, he resumed his duties as pastor of Calvary Baptist Church. But he did not forget his dream. By the early 1950s, under Reverend Robert Sneyd's leadership, skilled workmen who had recently immigrated from Italy had begun work on a new sanctuary for the church building of 1929, made from Port Credit limestone. In a tower over the main entrance, the artist Ernest Taylor created a memorial window, with two panels made from the broken glass Major Sneyd had collected and carefully packed in shell canisters. Joined by a mullion, the lancet panels include fragments from ninety-one cathedrals, churches, synagogues, and chapels of war-torn Europe, including Germany.

In need of money to pay the artist, Reverend Sneyd recalled a little-used army regulation dating back to the First World War, which gave a daily allowance to officers travelling without a servant (or batman). Going through proper channels, he obtained this allowance for a wide assortment of his wartime fellow officers, who in turn donated their share to pay for the window.

Canterbury, Coventry, and Exeter are only three of the many English cathedrals and churches represented in the memorial window that still distinguishes Calvary Baptist in east Toronto today. The figure of a king offering frankincense came from Chichester Cathedral. One panel contains a small cross from Rocquancourt Church in France. Perhaps the most poignant shard that Major Sneyd collected came from Normandy. It recalls the painful memory of burying a dozen Canadian soldiers of the Black Watch Regiment, along with those of enemy forces, whose bodies lay in a farmer's field near a small, shattered church. Another single piece, with a beautiful Head of Christ painted on the glass, came from the Dutch Roman Catholic Cathedral in 'S-Hertogenbosh. Whenever Reverend Sneyd saw the light shining through that face in the memorial window, it reminded him of the day that one of the Roman Catholic priests had given him a rosary to place in the hands of dying Catholic soldiers.

The inside of the 1953 church sanctuary is made from the limestone ballast in the holds of the returning ships that had transported supplies to Britain during the war. Major Sneyd had admired the beautiful, creamy stone that was quarried near Bath in England. After he arrived back in Canada, he arranged to have some of it brought to Toronto. The inside walls and arches of the new sanctuary, all built from this stone, give the interior a quiet, pristine atmosphere. Here, after the cataclysmic hell of war, one has a sense of peace. Sunlight streams through the plain mullioned windows of the walls onto the soft green carpeting. Tiny fossils, which are buried deep in the limestone, glint in the light and lend a sense of timelessness. The only colour present is from the stained glass window over the altar and the memorial window over the entrance. Drooping as if in mourning, on the right side of the memorial window hangs a Union Jack — the flag used by Major Sneyd throughout the war, in his funeral services for those who would not return.

Standing beneath the memorial window at Calvary Baptist today, one's eyes are focussed on the serene faces of children and then, caught by the fluidity of the scene, they are carried up to the light. Giving relief to the uniformed figures of the dead, bright butterflies, representing the "Flight to Glory," flit around golden sunflowers. Culminating with the figure of Christ, the onlooker has progressed through life, through destruction, to peace, and ultimately to the spiritual and omnipotent. It all makes an appropriate cenotaph for those who gave their lives so that future generations in Canada might carry on, strong and free.

Renfrew County

44. St. Mary's Roman Catholic Church, 1937
Highway 60, Wilno, east of Barry's Bay

Thus Saith the Lord: Let My People go ...
That they May Serve Me.
Exodus 8:1

Far away from any major urban centre, a traveller on Ontario Highway 60 south of Algonquin Park is astonished to see a solitary, magnificent edifice perched on a height of land above the road. Overlooking the Madawaska Valley, a scenic area of forests, lakes, and undulating hills, St. Mary's Roman Catholic Church near the hamlet of Wilno, in Renfrew County, marks a historic centre for the Polish community in present-day Ontario. It is not true that the multicultural society has all its roots in the urban areas of the twentieth century. The present St. Mary's building dates back to the late 1930s, just before the Second World War. But immigrants from the Kaszuby region in Poland had arrived in rural Renfrew County as early as 1858.

Towards the end of the eighteenth century, Poland lost its independence and was partitioned by Russia, Austria, and Prussia. The Kaszubs, who had their own language and customs, were assigned to the Prussian sector. True Polish nationalists, the Kaszubs became the object of Prussian oppression, both politically and economically. Ultimately the Prussian government launched a campaign to Germanize the Kaszubs, who were determined to retain their own language, faith, and traditions. In this atmosphere, successive small groups of Kaszubs were quick to answer advertisements calling for immigrants to settle along the Opeongo Colonization Road in Canada West during the late 1850s and early 1860s — in the still quite dense and rocky wilderness of the Madawaska Valley. The land in which they came to settle was much like the one that they had left behind. The Madawaska Valley had the same landscape of rolling hills and numerous lakes and rivers tucked into valleys as their former homeland in Polish Pomerania.

In the decades that followed, the hardy and industrious Kaszubs flourished and achieved at least a kind of economic stability in a very rugged environment. They toiled to clear rocks and boulders from the shallow, sandy soil. The snaking stone fences in the area today bear mute witness to the struggles of a pioneer people. As the old-timers said, "If rocks would sell, we would all be rich by now." As in their former land (which also had poor, sandy soil), the Kaszubs would turn to the forests as a source of income. Lumbering became their chief industry.

Because of its relative isolation from the outside world, the Kaszub community in the Madawaska Valley was able to retain many of its Polish customs. Above all, it remained strongly tied to the Roman Catholic Church. When the Kaszubs first arrived in the area, they had to rely on an Irish-born priest. During confession, language presented a major barrier. The innovative priest was able to overcome the difficulty by holding the penitent's hand while the interpreter asked questions. To acknowledge a specific sin, the penitent would give the priest's hand a squeeze. More Kaszubs would arrive as the nineteenth century wore on. As the settlements grew, Polish priests moved in as well. One settlement was centred around the parish church of St. Stanislaus Kostka in Hagarty Township. The parish priest, Father Ludwik Debski, would name the growing community Wilno, after his home town in Poland.

The Kaszub community in the Madawaska Valley would prove unusually resilient. Well into the twentieth century, in 1936, St. Stanislaus Kostka Roman Catholic Church in the hamlet of Wilno was destroyed in a fire. The same year, a new church of brick and stone was begun, blessed under the name of Mary, Queen of Poland. The resulting impressive St. Mary's Roman Catholic Church, which still surprises the traveller on Highway 60, was completed in 1937. A present-day visitor may pause beside the grotto of Our Lady of Lourdes which was later built into the terrace at the side of the church.

A walk through what is said to be the oldest Polish cemetery in Canada, adjacent to St. Mary's at Wilno, gives one a glimpse into the past of this unique community. Beside the newer graves are simple, well-weathered crosses from bygone days. These are the markers of vaults that were floored and lined with cement. The plots were then filled with earth and sodded over. Many of the inscriptions on the monuments are in the Kaszubian dialect and, when translated, reveal a longing for the homeland like that felt by immigrants from such places as Ireland or England or Scotland or many other parts of the world. At the end of the Second World War another influx of Polish immigrants arrived in the Madawaska Valley. Among them was a survivor of a German concentration camp, Father Stanislaw Kadziolka, who became pastor of St. Mary's Church.

Other Polish Catholic churches in and around the area are worth a visit today. In a less impressive setting than St. Mary's at Wilno, St. Hedwig's Church in Barry's Bay is located on a clearing that once served as a first peoples' meeting place. At a secluded

St. Mary's Roman Catholic Church, Wilno.

spot in the woods on the shore of Wadsworth Lake, the Chapel of Our Lady of the Angels was built by a former Polish army chaplain who was part of the assault on Monte Casino in Italy. On the main altar inside is a picture of the Madonna of Swarzewo, patroness of Kaszubian fishermen. To accommodate large numbers of summer visitors, an outdoor chapel, known as the Cathedral of the Pines has been constructed to celebrate Sunday Mass. Towering pine trees form a natural dome for the faithful who come to adore the Madonna. Remnants of the Polish custom of building roadside kapliczkis, or very small chapels, may be observed around Wadsworth Lake. (These were usually rough log structures where passersby could stop for a moment of prayer. It was also the custom to place handmade crosses and pictures of saints near crossroads in the area.)

Today many of the early Polish immigrants' descendants have left this rural area in Renfrew County. But they return from time to time. For other more recent Polish immigrants to the urban areas of Ontario, "Kaszuby" south of Algonquin Park has become a summer-vacation community. Many who no longer live in the area year-round are still caught up in the legend of the "Land of the Great Forest" in the Madawaska Valley, passed on by the first peoples to the hard-working Kaszubs from across the sea. For anyone who can sense the irresistible spell of the valley and appreciate its continuing wilderness charm and beauty, it is a kind of spiritual paradise. St. Mary's Church at Wilno is still helping to keep the legend of the paradise alive.

City of Toronto

45. Greek Orthodox Church of St. George, 1938 (1897)
115 Bond Street, Yonge & Dundas

> *To know or tell the origin of the divinities is beyond us,*
> *and we must accept the traditions of men of old time*
> *who affirm themselvesto be the offspring of the gods.*
> Plato (circa 429–347 B.C.)

*I*n 1938, the year after St. Mary's Roman Catholic Church in the Madawaska Valley was completed, the Jewish congregation of Holy Blossom Temple in Toronto had moved to its handsome new building on Bathurst Street. Its old building of 1897 on Bond Street, with two high domes highlighted against the downtown skyline, was left behind. The classical Byzantine style of the Bond Street building, however, appealed to the early pioneers of the city's twentieth-century Greek Orthodox community. The leaders of the community purchased the building, for what became the new Greek Orthodox Church of St. George.

There were still only a few thousand people from Greece in the Toronto of the late 1930s. The great majority of the present much larger Greek community in the metropolis arrived after the Second World War. Whenever they came, the new arrivals were descendants of one of the great ancient cultures of the world. Homer, Plato, Aristotle, Sophocles, and such figures had invented much of what was still being carried forward by the British and other European empires, well into the twentieth century. Classical Athens was a major inspiration for the republican ideals of the new United States of America. The first recorded Olympic games had been held in ancient Greece, in 776 B.C., and the same games had already been revived for the modern world in 1896, through the efforts of Greek nationalists and a French sportsman.

Before Christianity, the Greeks were polytheistic and pagan. Legend tells that Athena, goddess of wisdom and the arts, had originally competed with Poseidon for the possession of Athens. Poseidon struck the ground with his trident and a stream of salt water gushed forth. The wise and practical Athena gave the people a more utilitarian offering, an olive tree, and they named their city Athens, after her. Many other ancient

152

Toronto's Greek Orthodox Church of St. George.

Greek gods resided on Mount Olympus. Zeus, described by Homer as the god of all mortals, was also the god of weather and the dispenser of good and evil. The sanctuary of the Delphic Oracle was dedicated to Zeus's son, Apollo, who had special talents for prophecy.

As time went on, the Greeks had become more familiar with Jewish monotheism. It has been suggested that Plato's related conception of the absolute, eternal deity helped prepare the way for the acceptance of the Jewish sect of Christianity among the Gentiles. After the Roman emperor Constantine accepted Christianity in the fourth century, the Greeks became Christians, like everyone else in the empire. Yet, just as the empire itself would split into western and eastern parts, by 1054 Christianity had become irreparably divided into Western (Catholic) and Eastern (Orthodox) Churches. The Eastern Orthodox Church has always maintained that it was the Roman Catholic Church which drew apart from the one true faith. Even today, the two churches have as many similarities as differences.

One important difference is the refusal of the Eastern Orthodox Church, which considers Christ its ultimate leader, to accept one mere human being, such as the Roman Catholic Pope, as head of the Church. Only the Church itself is infallible, and the Holy Spirit comes from the Father. Mary, the mother of Jesus, is honoured above all other saints but not deified. She was cleansed at the time of the Annunciation and, by the grace of God, is without sin. The Nicene Creed is the official creed accepted by the

Orthodox Church and Orthodoxy worships one God in the Trinity, and the Trinity in unity.

The earlier twentieth-century Toronto Greek Orthodox community that moved into the old Holy Blossom Temple on Bond Street in 1938 inevitably made some changes in the building as time went on. The original menorah and inscription above the entrance was replaced by an elaborate mosaic of St. George slaying the mythical dragon. Much loved by the Greek people, St. George, who was an officer in the Roman army, is also a patron saint of the Greek Army. The imagery no doubt made sense as well for recent immigrants who were concerned to fit into a wider community that already honoured St. George as a patron saint of England — especially towards the end of the internationally troubled decade that led to the Second World War.

More important changes took place within the sanctuary. Today all indoor evidence of the old synagogue has been replaced by Orthodox symbols. The inside of the church was transformed by outstanding murals on the walls and the dome. Two monks, Theophilos and Chrysostomos, were brought from a monastery on Mount Athos in Greece to work on the elaborate paintings, over a period of seven years. The colours had to be specially blended from natural substances. Filling the entire dome, a magnificent likeness of Christ is set in brilliant colour. An elaborate screen, with icons or images of Jesus and Mary and various saints of the Orthodox Church, rests in front of the altar. Patron St. George has his place on Mary's right. The oldest icon in the church, a silver portrayal of the Holy Mother and the Infant Jesus, contrasts sharply with the intensity of the wall paintings done in the traditional Byzantine style.

There are as many as two dozen Greek Orthodox churches serving a Greek community of more than 100,000 people in the Greater Toronto Area today. But St. George's downtown remains a special place. As the architectural historian Eric Arthur said in the 1960s, anyone who cares to look will still "find this little bit of Byzantium on Bond Street an interesting and colourful discovery."

District of Cochrane

46. Christ the King Cathedral (Roman Catholic), 1947
Moosonee

> *I will praise you among the nations, O Lord!*
> Psalms 57:9

A surviving sign of Ontario's ultimately disappointed grand enthusiasm for its far north in the earlier twentieth century is what is now known as the Ontario Northland Railway, which connects the urban areas of the south with the province's only salt water port, at Moosonee on James Bay. With construction starting in 1903 at North Bay (already well connected by rail with Ottawa and Toronto), the railway finally reached Moosonee in July 1932, in the depths of the Great Depression. This prompted the Roman Catholic Church to establish a mission headquarters in the village and, following a period of evolution which was at least somewhat shorter than that of the railway itself, the present Christ the King Cathedral in Moosonee was finally erected after the Second World War, in 1947.

Even today, the true north of the old Indian and European fur trade is still evident in Moosonee — fifteen miles up the Moose River from James Bay. The name of the village comes from the Cree word "Moosoneek," which means "at the Moose." Both Moosonee and the adjacent Moose Factory Island are situated on the tidewaters of James Bay. Summer tides can reach one and a half metres with about six hours between high and low tides.

Following Henry Hudson's harsh voyage of 1610, another explorer, Thomas James, had penetrated into the lower part of Hudson Bay and called it James Bay, after himself. In 1686, concerned about the activities of the English Hudson's Bay Company in the area, Pierre Le Moyne d'Iberville overran the Company's forts and claimed the region on behalf of the King of France. An era of recurrent bloody battles between the French and the English followed, until the Treaty of Utretcht confirmed the area for the British Crown in 1713.

Christ the King Cathedral, Moosonee.

In a different world, almost two centuries later, in 1903, the Revillon Frères Trading Company of Paris established a post at Moosonee, to compete with the Hudson's Bay Company post across the river at Moose Factory. Thousands of years earlier, the area had been settled by the Swampy Cree, who kept in touch with their fellow Algonkian-speaking peoples to the south through complex networks of canoe waterways. The Cree still constitute the majority of the 3000 people who live in both Moosonee and Moose Factory today.

There are still no roads leading into Moosonee. Until the arrival of the railway in 1932, the village was at least eight to ten days away from the nearest more southerly centre by canoe and portage (or longer again by snowshoe in the winter). It is now a gateway to the larger Hudson Bay area, and a departure point for plane and boat travel into the northern bush. It is still possible to reach Moosonee by canoe or snowshoe, but present-day access is usually by aircraft or an Ontario Northland excursion train from Cochrane known as the Polar Bear Express.

Leaving Cochrane early in the morning, the Express takes four hours to wind its way across 186 miles of sparsely populated forest, muskeg, wetland, and scrub brush. The first part of the journey passes through the northern Clay Belt, which has fertile land but not the agricultural potential that was once hoped for. Crossing the Abitibi River, a once-great site of the logging industry comes into view. From there, thousands of cords of black spruce were shipped to pulp mills down south. A fire ravaged 30,000 acres of adjacent forest in 1976.

Leaving the end of the road system behind at Fraserdale, the train slows for a view of the huge, fully automated generating station at the Otter Rapids Dam. The waters of James and Hudson Bays once covered one of the world's largest wetlands — an area roughly eight hundred miles long, varying in width from one hundred to 250 miles. A permafrost region, black spruce, sphagnum moss, and lichen grow In the marshes while sedges, dwarf birch, and tamarack grow in the fens. Stands of white spruce and birch, Balsam fir, and trembling aspen grow along well-drained river banks. Before reaching the end of its journey, the Polar Bear Express rumbles across an upside-down bridge. The supporting girders, instead of being underneath the bridge, are on top to allow ice chunks free passage during the spring thaw. Arriving in Moosonee, the traveller is greeted by a goose, a symbol of Cree culture, emblazoned on the local water tower.

Although there are still no roads leading into Moosonee, vehicles, mostly pickup trucks and buses, are transported into the village by train. Boats, now powered by motors, are still the common method of transportation between Moosonee and Moose Factory Island, but an ice bridge links the two communities in winter. Crossing a wide expanse of the Moose River, giant snowplows keep this route passable for the school bus to transport pupils from Moose Factory to the high school in Moosonee. When the ice begins to break up and the river is not safe for either bus or boat transport, the pupils are flown across by helicopter.

The first Mass on the shores of James Bay was celebrated in 1672 by Father Albanel, and the Oblate Missionaries began a ministry in the area in 1847. But it wasn't until the railway reached Moosonee in 1932 that the Roman Catholic mission established a headquarters there. In 1939 the Holy See created the Apostolic Vicarate of Moosonee — a vast area covering 1.2 million square kilometres. The Apostolic Vicarate became the Diocese of Moosonee in 1967.

In keeping with aboriginal tradition and the name Moosonee, a stained glass window of a moose graces the arca above the entrance to the present-day Christ the King Cathedral, which was built in 1947. When the cathedral underwent renovations in 1987, Detlef Gotzens created new stained-glass windows, from the work of the Cree artisan, Keena. In a window on the west side of the nave, on a backdrop of northern woods and water, a caring Jesus is watching while a Cree man and woman haul in nets of fish.

In another stained glass window, to commemorate his visits to Ontario in 1984 and 1987, Pope John Paul II's figure is illuminated by the light of the Spirit, as, one presumes, the Huron chief at the Martyrs' Shrine far to the south presents him with the Eagle feather of peace. A stylized goose above the Holy Father's head symbolizes freedom. As though they were hands, snowshoes seem to be raised in supplication. Beneath the snowshoes is a deadfall trap, a requisite for fur trapping which has been an independent way of life for generations of Cree.

On the east side of the chancel, a birchbark canoe is trapped in glass. Kateri Tekakwitha (1656–1680), the Mohawk Virgin who was beatified in 1980, is pictured with the Cross, symbol of Christianity. A child of an Algonquin mother and a Mohawk father, Kateri is surrounded by three medallions: a deer representing her mother's clan; a turtle, symbol of the Mohawks; and an eagle, characterizing the protective Spirit. Another window portrays a beautiful scene of the nativity. The faces of the Holy Family are Cree. Natural enemies, the lynx, owl, and snowshoe hare abide side by side in peace. A tikinakun or aboriginal cradle completes the picture.

With the recent sale of the Catholic church at Moose Factory to the island's Anglican majority, Christ the King Cathedral in Moosonee is now the only Roman Catholic house of worship in the area. At Mass in the cathedral today, one should not be surprised to hear the service read and the hymns sung in the Cree language. Almost four centuries after "European contact," James Bay remains a rugged northern frontier, of sometimes striking natural beauty. Just what it may ultimately develop into is still one of Ontario's great mysteries.

Lambton County

47. Christ Church (Anglican), 1959

Petrolia, southeast of Sarnia

> *A small town of many churches.*
> Elizabeth Luther (1924–)

$\mathcal{B}$ack down south, far away from Moosonee, the rural and small town Ontario that dominated the nineteenth century had, in some undeniable ways, shrunk to a pale imitation of its former self by the later part of the twentieth century. When Verschoyle Benson Blake and Ralph Greenhill published their interesting book, *Rural Ontario*, in the late 1960s, they noted how they "intended to record an aspect of the older-settled rural parts of Ontario, an aspect now being rapidly eroded by changing conditions."

In other ways, there have been many places where the old rural and small town life — along with the central role it assigns to the local church — has adjusted to changing conditions and carried on, quite successfully. A place of just this sort is the Town of Petrolia in Lambton County, in the southwestern part of the province, not far to the south and east of Sarnia.

One of the various present-day specialties of Petrolia is interesting churches. Another is the total number of churches now serving fewer than five thousand souls. Nine churches of different denominations call the faithful to service every week. Why does such a small town have this many churches — some of which are large enough to seat a thousand people?

The answer has a lot to do with the community's unique and, to many people, still surprising history as an early centre of the oil industry in North America. Although Pennsylvanians like to think that their state was the birthplace of the industry, Lambton County in the old Canada West upstaged them. A decade before Canadian confederation, James Williams, a carriage maker by trade, dug a hole on his property near what is now called Oil Springs, a short distance south of Petrolia, and discovered black gold. By 1858 he had established the first successful oil well in North America. Although the market for oil then was not what it would later become, it was big enough to change the future of the surrounding area overnight.

In this previously unheard of swampy, peculiar-smelling, unattractive part of the world two small boom towns, Oil Springs and Petrolia, mushroomed. Oil was actually discovered in what is now Petrolia in 1861, and wells were being developed there when the place was incorporated in 1866. (Originally meant to be called "Petrolea," a clerical error changed the official spelling.) For various reasons, Petrolia soon outstripped Oil Springs in importance and growth. Soon the new residents of the rising community began to build churches.

The Presbyterians were the first and had their church constructed before Petrolia had even been given a name. The Methodists were not to be overshadowed by their Presbyterian brethren. Both Wesleyan and Episcopalian Methodists built churches within a stone's throw of each other, then vied for members. Meanwhile both the Baptists and the Roman Catholics had organized congregations and built churches. The Anglicans soon followed. In later years other denominations would join the crowd.

Petrolia flourished over the next several decades. By 1880 several refiners in the area had merged to form the Imperial Oil Company. For a time there was extra money in the town, and it still shows in some of the buildings that have been bequeathed to the twentieth century. With the advent of a new railway and the construction of a bridge over the creek, there was a shift in the settlement pattern. In order to accommodate their congregations, the churches moved, one by one, to an area known as "the flats" — an unsuitable place where the land flooded each spring. Then, in 1884, the two main Methodist bodies joined together to form one Methodist church. The congregations rejoiced and decided to build a new, united house of worship in a better location. The Presbyterians would also move from the flats into what is now the centre of Petrolia.

Elaborate interiors grace the largest old churches in the town today. St. Paul's United (formerly Methodist) was built with a semi-circular seating pattern — an innovative concept for its time. First Baptist Church has floor-to-ceiling pocket doors that provide extra space whenever the faithful overflow the main body of the church. A beautiful wrought-iron balcony circles the upper level of St. Andrew's Presbyterian Church. Built of the same yellow brick used in many of the buildings in this part of southwestern Ontario, St. Philip's Roman Catholic Church is smaller than its Protestant neighbours — a reflection of the Protestant predominance in much of nineteenth-century Ontario, that has since diminished.

In the midst of such a heritage, the present Christ Church (Anglican) in Petrolia enjoys the distinction of having been built as recently as 1959. It is said that the first Anglicans arrived in the old oil boom town in 1866. They were few in number, and held

Christ Church, Petrolia.

their first services in the bar room of a local hotel. In 1882 their first structure, built ten years earlier, was replaced by a beautiful white brick church. The members of the congregation continued to worship in this lovely edifice until 1957 when, as in so many other cases, fire struck and completely destroyed their house of worship.

The undaunted community rallied and a new Christ Church rose from the ashes. As a sign of just how well the community has continued to remember its own heritage, the interesting stained glass window includes an oil motif. Christ, in his role as shepherd of His flock, is surrounded by a fly wheel, the device that generates energy for the jerker line which draws oil from various parts of the field. Thus the fly wheel symbolizes the divinity of Christ. Surrounding the fly wheel are four stages of the petroleum industry. A jerker line at the base of the window records significant dates in the industry and the life of the Petrolia area.

With the gradual development of more profitable oil wells in the United States, the price of oil dropped and, although the wells of Lambton County continued to produce, the great boom era in Petrolia came to an end. The population dropped from over ten thousand to its present level of just under five thousand. In one sense it all happened a long time ago now. Yet the place has retained something of its historic hustle and bustle. When driving through today, one still catches the pungent, lingering smell of oil. It doesn't come from the light standards, which are facsimiles of oil derricks, but from occasional backyards where there are still small oil wells pumping black gold into an adjacent barrel.

The more recent and present-day community has also been concerned to keep up many of the expansive old structures which the long-since-vanished boom bequeathed. The railway is gone, but the train station remains intact as the local library. The newly refurbished yellow brick town hall — completely gutted by fire in 1989 and restored after much controversy — is a testimonial to a people as determined as their ancestors to ensure that the place where they live will remain a place worth noting. Known as Victoria Hall, the building dates back to 1889. It originally housed municipal offices, police and fire stations, a jail, and an opera house with remarkable acoustics. The restored structure was re-opened with a gala event in September 1992. It is now home to the town's administrative offices, along with a 425-seat climate-controlled theatre (which presented three off-Broadway comedies for its summer 2000 season).

On a Sunday morning, streams of people from Petrolia and the surrounding country-side still fill the many seats in the churches of this progressive Old Ontario small town, that has somehow learned how to carry its old virtues on into the changing world of today. It is as if the place is reminding us that, in changing ways, this too is a part of the future, just as it was of the past.

Pioneers Today

The later part of the twentieth century in Ontario has seen some remarkable changes. Even in their wildest dreams, the pioneers of old Upper Canada could not have envisioned the province today. But neither the Huron nor the Jesuits in the prelude to the fur trade could have envisioned what Ontario became in the nineteenth century either. The world keeps changing, and there is no sign at the moment that the change will stop soon.

Over the past several decades, exciting advances in technology have finally taken us into a new era of jet-set travel, microelectronic computers, and talking over cell phones on the street. Along with a great decline in the old rural social and economic dominance, electricity and everything it now brings with it has come to rural Ontario. Those who struggled with the rugged corduroy and even just plain dirt roads of Upper Canada would marvel at the province's highway system in the early twenty-first century.

One interesting feature of life in Ontario today is that the birth rates of the aboriginal First Nations are currently greater than those of the province at large. Continuing advances in technology have also brought what Marshall McLuhan of St. Michael's College at the University of Toronto christened the global village in the 1960s. This has brought even more striking changes in earlier patterns of immigration. From the early seventeenth down to the end of the nineteenth centuries, most new arrivals from across the sea came from the more northern and western parts of Europe. By the earlier twentieth century the net had begun to widen, to include various people from the more southern and eastern parts of Europe. In the later twentieth century it widened again, to take in people from virtually all parts of the world. New kinds of pioneers have come flocking into the province, on new kinds of ships that fly through the air.

Although people of African descent, from the United States, had been among the early pioneers of Upper Canada and Canada West, much larger numbers have arrived in Ontario in the 1960s, 1970s, 1980s, and 1990s — from the West Indies (where Lieutenant Governor Simcoe had gone, after he left Upper Canada), from the United States again, and from various parts of Africa. They have brought their own contributions to the province's deepening mixed community. In many cases they have also brought roots entangled in the old united empire to which Ontario has traditionally been so loyal — an empire which itself survives vaguely in the present-day Commonwealth of Nations, side by side with the North American Free Trade Agreement.

Other new Ontario pioneers from various parts of Asia (and Africa and the Middle East) have come from similar entanglements with the old global empire — in the former Raj in South Asia, and such other places as Singapore and Hong Kong. Many of these new pioneers have also brought with them their often ancient great religions from the Old World beyond Europe. The most striking signs of this fresh spiritual ferment are still in the new economic heartland of the sprawling Greater Toronto Area. But already it has started to move further afield.

In some other respects, the province at large is more secular than it used to be. According to the most recent Canadian census of religion, in 1991, more than twelve percent of Ontario's almost twelve million people claimed to have "No religious affiliation." Yet that leaves a quite overwhelming majority who still officially identify with one or another established form of the life of the spirit. Traditional Protestant Christians still account for the single largest group (just under 45 percent of the total provincial population, according to the 1991 census), followed by Catholics (Roman, Ukrainian, and Other), at just over 35 percent. Eastern Orthodox Christians are at a much smaller 1.9 percent, and people the statisticians now call Jewish (as opposed to the "Hebrew" of an earlier official language) are at 1.8 percent.

At the sharpest edge of change, what the statisticians call "eastern non-Christian" religions were adhered to by almost four percent of the province-wide population in 1991. Any more recent trip through the central parts of southern Ontario suggests that this number will be considerably larger in the forthcoming census of 2001. These are the newest spiritual pioneers in the province today. They are building new houses of worship in the architectural styles of their homelands.

One sometimes can't help but wonder just where all the new diversity in the old mixed community will lead. There are signs that the newest spiritual pioneers are stimulating the life of the spirit in the province at large, in all its old and new forms. The old Ontario, long used to parades of kilted Scots and Irish, and then treated to a course in Italian cuisine, has most recently seen its community life brightened by processions of Chinese dragons, and the sunny rhythms of the Caribbean. In the Greater Toronto Area of the early twenty-first century, the vibrations of temple chimes, the cries of the muezzin, and the unique sound of the shophar mingle with the ringing of old church bells. Their clearest message is that, in the life of the spirit as in so much else, Ontario is going to have a very interesting future.

Greater Toronto Area

48. Gurdwara Shromani Sikh Society
269 Pape Avenue, south of Gerrard, Toronto

49. Gurdwara Ontario Khalsa Dar Bar, 1979
7080 Dixie Road, at Derry Road, Mississauga, Peel Region

He who submits to the will of God,
is accepted and treasured by Him.
Guru Nanak (circa 1469–1539)

*W*edged between their neighbours on Pape Avenue in the Toronto inner city, the local followers of one of the world's newer religions chose two semi-detached houses for their first home in their new country. Like other pioneers before them, back in the early days of the 1960s they had to adapt a building originally intended for something else to the purposes of a house of worship. Only the name above the entrance distinguishes the premises of the Gurdwara Shromani Sikh Society from other houses on the street.

As the Sikh community in the wider region increased in numbers, a larger and more appropriate place of worship was required. In 1979, work on the 135,000-square-foot Khalsa Dar Bar Temple on Dixie Road in Mississauga began, on 1.8 acres of land. Today this gathering place for Toronto-area Sikhs is still being expanded, on 38 acres of land. The Sikh Holy Scripture is installed in the main hall of the temple. Every person, irrespective of caste, creed, culture, or sex can visit. On entering the hall, every one bows in reverence. Both men and women may conduct the service which begins with the singing of hymns accompanied by musical instruments.

Sikhism, placing sole emphasis on God as the Impersonal Absolute, is the latest flowering of Hindu mysticism. Born in 1469 around Talwandi, about thirty miles from Lahore (in present-day Pakistan, right next to the Punjab in India), the founder of Sikhism was Nanak Nirakari. The name Nanak has spiritual significance and means servant of the "Formless One." A contemporary of Martin Luther, Nanak also questioned certain practices perpetrated in the name of religion. But unlike Luther, who did not want to

Gurdwara Shromani Sikh Society, Toronto.

separate from his church, Nanak became the first Guru of an entirely new religion.

Like Jesus in the temple, Nanak also reacted to the religious dogmas of his time and place when he was very young. When the priest attempted to place the janeu, or sacred thread, around his neck, the boy seized the thread and questioned its usefulness. When the priest explained that, without the thread Nanak would always be seen as a low-caste person, Nanak replied, "Make mercy your cotton, contentment your thread, continence its knot, truth its twist. That would be a janeu for the soul."

Under pressure from his parents, Nank married at the age of sixteen and his wife bore him two sons. To support them, he worked as a storekeeper in the service of the government. There he met Mardana, a wandering minstrel, who became his lifelong companion.

At the age of thirty-eight, Nanak had an extraordinary and deeply moving spiritual experience. During his morning bath in the river, he was taken in a vision into God's presence. Here he was told: "Go and repeat my name and cause others to do so. Live uncontaminated by the world. Practice the repetition of my name, charity, ablutions, worship, and meditation." Nanak described himself as a God-intoxicated man who had lost his reason in pursuit of the Lord. Thereupon he gave away all his possessions to the poor and began his life as a wandering preacher, accompanied by his companion Mardana.

Accepted as the greatest work in Punjabi literature, the *Adi Granth* (a collection of Sikh sacred scriptures) owes its existence to the fifth Guru, Arjun, who compiled it from the writings of many different authors. Likened to the Bible, it is an anthology of

Gurdwara Ontario Khalsa Dar Bar, Mississauga.

devotional outpourings that have been drawn from both the Hindu and Muslim traditions of modern India. An authoritative book of more than 1400 pages, it propagates the ideal of one universal faith, a worldwide religion that cuts across the borders of caste and creeds. Like the Christian Scriptures, the *Adi Granth* preaches the fatherhood of God and the brotherhood of man. It gives prime importance to the attainment of spiritual greatness by following the path of truthful living, contentment, and humility. It calls for devotion and complete surrender to the will of God.

Sikhism has no rituals and no deities to be worshipped. God is supreme. The only religious object to be found in the Golden Temple at Amritsar, the sanctum sanctorum of the Sikh world, in the Punjab in India, is the *Adi Granth*. In the mornings it is dressed in brocade and placed on a throne under a jewelled canopy. At night it rests on a golden bed. Every day, constantly waving a fly-whisk over the book, priests read it continuously. It is said that this pattern has been uninterrupted since 1577.

The great majority of Sikhs in Ontario today, as in Canada at large, have come from a network of villages in the Punjab ("Land of the Five Rivers"). Sikhs account for as little as two percent of the present-day population in India itself. They nevertheless wield much power and influence in Indian society, especially in the civil service and the army. Most Sikhs in Ontario belong to the Khalsa order which identifies adult males through five *kakas* or K's: *kes* (uncut hair and beard), *kirpan* (dagger), *kara* (steel bracelet), *khanga* (comb), and *kach* (undercloth). Although some Sikh men shave and cut their hair, they are considered unqualified to wear the five Ks.

Coming from a traditionally close family system, Sikhs in Canada have had to adjust to a legal and economic environment that encourages the independence of individual family members. Concerned with *izzat*, the honour and respectability of keeping up the good name of the family, they have been challenged by a more open and permissive society. At the same time, Canadian governments have accommodated at least some Sikh traditions by allowing the wearing of turbans in Canadian military and police forces.

At the old inner-city temple on Pape Avenue in Toronto today, a *Granthi* (reader) officiates at the Sunday morning service. The only embellishments in the plain interior are streamers radiating from the overhead lights. A long strip of carpet divides the floor space in front of the rostrum. Women in traditional clothing are seated on the left and the men, most of whom are in western dress, are seated on the right. All must wear head coverings.

As is common in Sikh temples, the much more expansive Khalsa Dar Bar in suburban Mississauga has a community kitchen (*Gur-Ka-Langar*), which provides food to all devotees, pilgrims, and visitors. Funded by contributions of Toronto-area Sikhs and open twenty-four hours a day, it is a place of equality where everyone, opulent or poor, educated or lowly, king or peasant, shares the same food. Being seated on the floor in one row is a sign of humility and togetherness. As soon as possible, newborn children of Sikh families are brought into the temple to be blessed and named. The Holy Book is opened randomly and the infant given a name beginning with the first initial on the page.

A Sikh is expected to rise every morning before dawn and, after bathing, to meditate on the Name of God. Through meditation, the Sikh attempts to become one with God. This also requires the performance of duty to both family and society. It is a religion that exhorts people to strive for improvement. Ultimately, and in a way that is similar enough to other religions in Ontario today, Sikhism deals with the relationships among God, humans, and the universe, emphasizing the belief in one Supreme Being, the Creator. Every Sikh prayer ends with the request: "Through Nanak may the glory of your Name increase and may the whole world be blessed by your Grace."

York Region

50. Hindu Temple Society of Canada (Ganesh Mandir), 1983
10945 Bayview Avenue, at Elgin Mills Road, Richmond Hill

> In whatever name and form you worship Him,
> through that He will be realized by you.
> Sri Ramakrishna Paramahamsa (1836–1886)

For some time an impressive Ontario expression of the larger and much more ancient Hinduism from which the Sikhs themselves descend has been arising around the old village of Elgin Mills, north of the present-day City of Toronto in York Region.

All that remains of Elgin Mills (now part of Richmond Hill) is a street which bears its name. Back in the earlier nineteenth century, a toll road was constructed, east from Elgin Mills to Markham and Stouffville. The slow horse-drawn vehicles of the day had no escape from the human toll master. Today, just south of the area, the new Highway 407 toll road runs across the land. Various classes of automobile race over it at speeds that would have astounded the pioneers of Upper Canada. In many cases the toll master is an electronic device.

Gone are almost all the old pioneer homes. Mennonite "grossdoddy" houses, with accommodation for aged parents at one end of the structure, have given way to computer-age rows of solid, look-alike townhouses on small, grassy plots. On land that was settled by new arrivals from south of the Great Lakes almost two centuries ago, the latest new arrivals, from the old jewel of the empire on which the sun never set, are putting their roots down into the soil.

In 1983, members of the Hindu community in Toronto purchased a four-acre piece of land in the area. A new building, in an architectural style quite different from that of the Upper Canadian pioneers, began to rise on a small knoll beside the stream flowing through what had once been Elgin Mills. The outlines of a Hindu temple from the South Asian subcontinent began to take shape against the skyline of the Greater Toronto Area today.

Coming from a heterogeneous cultural and linguistic background themselves, Hindus form the single-largest religious group in modern India's own very diverse population. Since the late 1960s quite large numbers of Hindus have been arriving in Canada, and especially in Ontario, and even more especially in the Greater Toronto Area — hoping for better economic and educational opportunities in their new country.

Hindus from south and southeast Asia outside India itself have also been coming to Canada since the 1960s. Many have come from present-day Sri Lanka (the former Ceylon), an island nation off the southeast coast of India. Long known as "the pearl of the Indian Ocean," it is a land fringed by sandy beaches. Tea plantations abound on the mountainous interior. For much of the late twentieth century, protracted civil conflict between the majority Sinhalese (Buddhists) and the minority Tamils (Hindus) has unsettled life in Sri Lanka. Fleeing the strife, many Hindu Tamils have made their way to Ontario, and especially to the Greater Toronto Area.

Hinduism as a religion is a complex subject. Because of the plethora of forms it takes, the present-day government of India, seeking a legal definition, has simply designated a Hindu as someone accepted by his or her Hindu peers. Hinduism derives from a background both physically and culturally removed from the Judaeo-Christian tradition, and has even a radically different perspective from that of the traditional western world. Even those who have studied it for a lifetime do not feel they can summarize what it is in any short space.

It is certainly one of the most ancient religions still practiced today, and it can be said that in Hinduism God is both immanent and transcendent. God can be manifest in forms and without forms. In Hinduism, God without form is neither He nor She, but instead referred to as It. God is believed to have many incarnations and, as with the God of Judaism, the latest incarnation is yet to come. When it happens, God will come for the benefit of all humanity. All paths lead to God.

Unlike other world religions today, Hinduism is more of a sometimes bewildering variety of precepts than any fixed doctrine. It is not a tightly defined religion but rather the way of thought of an ancient civilization. There is no central figure of authority and no single, sacred book. Self is the source of all creativity. The various ideas and beliefs that make up Hinduism are not the result of any one person's work. One is not different from the universe, but an integral part of it. Although it is usual to regard everyone as a believer in the ultimate reality of God, even a belief of this sort is not an essential requirement of Hinduism.

Hinduism is also not a church-based religion. Hindus normally get together in a temple at festival time, and for sacraments and rituals. When required, counselling is provided by a guru. This generally takes the form of readings from a scripture such as

Drawing of the planned exterior of the Hindu Temple Society of Canada in Richmond Hill.

the *Gita*, which deals with fulfilling the duties of life in conformity with one's spiritual ability. No attempt is made to indoctrinate those being counselled in what is good or proper. Conviction must emerge from within the individual.

Traditionally, Hindu temples are built on the banks of a river. In Richmond Hill today the Ganesh Mandir structure that began to rise on a small knoll beside the stream flowing through what had once been Elgin Mills, in 1983, is thus suitably located, and the stream has become a *Theertha* or "Holy River." Built in the "*Agama*" tradition, with a worshipping area of over 18,000 square feet, this structure is the largest of its kind in North America. It houses three complete temples under one roof — one for Lord Vishnu, a second for Lord Murugan, and a third for Lord Ganesa. Brought from India, a team of fifteen sculptors created the artwork on the fourteen individual altars which house the deities of the Hindu pantheon.

Occupying a prominent position, Lord Ganesa, first son of Lord Siva, is the first deity to be worshipped by Hindus in any function or festival. Lord Murugan, second son of Lord Siva and commander-in-chief of the divine army, is the main deity worshipped by Tamil-speaking people around the world. Lord Siva, signifying the concept of God as formless or beyond any form that anyone can attribute to him, has a special place. The statue of him is said not to have been made by man, but to have been plucked directly from the holy waters of the Ganges River, and given to the Temple Society in Richmond Hill. Parvati, consort of Lord Siva, has her own altar.

As one moves across the vast floor area from the first to the second temple, majestic Vishnu bestows his divine grace on all devotees. Lakshmi, referred to as "Thayar" meaning the Mother, is the consort of Vishnu. She helps protect the lives of people in heaven and on earth. Along with the statues on these altars, there are numerous granite statues placed around the building. Smaller metal statues called Utsava moorthis are used in processions. At the start of the annual festival, a flag is hoisted for the main deity and lowered once the festival is over. During a festival as many as ten thousand people from surrounding parts of the Greater Toronto Area may visit Ganesh Mandir in Richmond Hill to worship.

The exterior of the building is still under construction. The art of erecting Hindu temples is a long process, with precise calculations, methods, and rules that have been followed for centuries. Also complicated by western technologies and building codes, the work on the outside has only just begun. When it is completed, there will be two main Royal Towers rising to eighty-two feet and three smaller towers about forty-five feet high. These resplendent towers, covered in gold leaf, will be visible to all who pass by. Landscaping will complement the finished exterior of the building, and preserve the natural setting of the flowing stream.

One might come away thinking again about the old Elgin Mills and the age of the Upper Canadian pioneers. The still much-remembered first lieutenant governor of Upper Canada, John Graves Simcoe, had wanted to crown his career with an appointment in India (the jewel of the empire, after all). But he died shortly after he finally received the appointment he wanted so much. Now India and its largest religion have arrived in the Upper Canada he left behind. Even in an age of computers and jet airplanes, the life of the spirit still moves in mysterious ways.

51. Cathedral of the Transfiguration (Byzantine Catholic), 1984
10350 Woodbine Avenue, near Elgin Mills Road, Markham

> *Take heed that ye do not your alms before men,*
> *to be seen of them: otherwise ye have no*
> *reward of your Father which is in heaven.*
> Matthew 6:1

There are of course still new Christian churches being built by various new pioneers in Ontario. But even here the most interesting stories have some novelty as well. One of these stories began on a warm day in August 1984, at a site in the present-day Town of Markham, somewhat to the east of Ganesh Mandir, along the old toll road from Elgin Mills. Accustomed enough to warm summer days, Pope John Paul II blessed the granite cornerstone of the new Cathedral of the Transfiguration — in the Byzantine-Slovak Eparchy of SS Cyril & Methodius of Canada.

The event is said to mark the first time that the cornerstone for such a building in the western hemisphere was blessed by a pope. Subsequently, a replica of a sixth-century Byzantine Catholic cathedral in eastern Europe has arisen, like some exotic illusion, on twelve acres of old Ontario farmland. It is designed in the traditional cruciform style with a nave crossed by a transept. Beneath the huge central dome, the floor slopes down to five steps that lead to the altar.

The building is entangled with the career of the late Stephen Roman — one of the success stories of the Toronto business community that emerged from the Great Depression of the 1930s. Stephen Roman arrived in Canada in 1937, a sixteen-year-old farm boy and high-school dropout from the Slovak part of Czechoslovakia. Without a penny in his pocket, he took a job as a tomato picker. But like many other new arrivals, he was hoping to find riches in his new country. More than most, he made his hopes real. From rags to riches, his was a true-life Horatio Alger saga. A tough-minded, hard-working individual, he turned some early shares of eight-and-a-half-cent mining stock into a multi-billion-dollar resource empire.

Coming from the troubled politics of central and eastern Europe in the late 1930s, Stephen Roman was a strong believer in democracy. Another of his admirable qualities was his devotion to the Byzantine Catholic Church in Canada. As suggested by the story of St. Peter's Church in Thunder Bay, some Slovak pioneers in Ontario have been ordinary Roman Catholics. Others have been more unusual Byzantine Catholics — or Eastern

The Cathedral during construction.

Orthodox Christians who nonetheless embrace full communion with the Church of Rome and its primate, Pope John Paul II, the successor of St. Peter. Believing that the most important thing in life was to be in a good position to meet one's creator, Stephen Roman started by donating land for a cathedral to serve Byzantine Catholics in the Greater Toronto Area. When asked what the cathedral would cost, he replied: "Christ said, 'You donate something and tell your friends, you've got your reward already, but do something and don't tell anyone, you get your reward in heaven.'"

An impressive structure designed in Slovakian style, the Cathedral of the Transfiguration that has since arisen in the northwestern part of present-day Markham is an enlarged replica of a church in Stephen Roman's homeland. The poured concrete walls are faced with granite slabs brought from Québec. Standing on the five-acre front lawn, one's attention is drawn to the three copper-clad domes. Rising above the main sanctuary, the 206-foot centre tower houses the world's largest peal of bells. They weigh a total of 71,000 pounds. On a muggy day in July 1986, Mr. Roman stood among a throng of spectators who filled the air with the singing of Slovak folk songs. He watched as a crane hoisted three bells through the opening of the tower. On hand to supervise the delicate installation, foundry owner Pierre Paccard, using a two-way radio, directed the crane operators as they inched the largest bell into place.

Cast in Annecy, France, the largest of the three bells weighs 37,000 pounds and qualifies as the second largest church bell in the world in its own right. It is named St. Stephen: the other two are named for St. Anne and the prophet Daniel. Pierre Paccard and his son personally supervised the casting of the bells in France, and stayed with them during their trip across the Atlantic Ocean and up the St. Lawrence Seaway. The Paccards then saw to the unloading of the bells at Toronto harbour, and their transportation on a flatbed truck to the site in Markham.

There, a day later, interested observers were awed by the colossal size of what the Paccards had brought. The centre bell, already in place, dwarfed the technicians who were struggling to hang the Daniel bell. Gleaming in the morning sun, it was finally hung in the belfry after a last manoeuvre. As a test for purity of pitch was performed, a deafening boom rang across the countryside. With his hands over his ears, Pierre Paccard signalled that all was well and his job was done.

Even today, the inside of the Cathedral of the Transfiguration in Markham remains unfinished. Sunlight shines through the plain glass lancet-style windows. Only the five-million-piece mosaic of glass and cera-

The Cathedral of the Transfiguration today.

mic brightens the stark interior. (Overlooking the sanctuary, this icon of the Virgin Mary occupies a central place in the art and theology of eastern Christianity.) At least one of Stephen Roman's hopes and ambitions has not yet been quite fulfilled.

The Cathedral has nonetheless already become a much-discussed landmark in the sprawling expanse of the Greater Toronto Area. Each Sunday the faithful chant the old liturgy of the Byzantine Catholic Church. The world's largest peal of bells resounds across the suburban countryside, in one of the world's various rising megapolitan regions. According to the now-retired Bishop Michael Rusnak, who gave the late Stephen Roman last rites and absolution, Mr. Roman's abiding words were: "Take care of the Cathedral."

City of Toronto

52. Islamic Foundation of Toronto, 1989
441 Nugget Avenue, north of Sheppard, Scarborough

> *How much greater is the joy and sense of wonder and*
> *miracle when the Qur'an opens our spiritual eyes! ...*
> *New worlds are opened out.*
> Abdullah Yusuf Ali (1872–1952)

Some distance southeast of the Byzantine Catholic Cathedral in Markham, down in the older suburban parts of what has recently become the new amalgamated City of Toronto, a time-traveller from the pioneer days of Upper Canada would no doubt be surprised to hear a new sound ascending heavenward. Five times a day the voice of an a muezzin calling the faithful to prayer rises above the roar of the constant automobile traffic at the nearby intersection of Nugget Avenue and Markham Road.

A large, pristine, white cement-stone building with a soaring minaret dominates the skyline. It is the regular religious home of two thousand people of the Islamic faith in the surrounding area. During *Eid* prayers the number can swell up to ten thousand.

Around the globe, members of the world's second-largest religion will also be paying obeisance. Five times each day, Muslims face Mecca to pray to Allah. Islam, a prophetic religion that shares an uncompromising monotheism with Christianity and Judaism, embraces some one billion adherents worldwide today. Although all followers of Islam enjoy a unity of faith in Allah, there are two major historical divisions, Sunni and Shia, each with somewhat different beliefs and practices. Worldwide, the great majority of Muslims are Sunni.

The Islamic religion was born in the seventh century. Muslims believe that worship of Allah was not evolutionary but rather a return to the forgotten past, to the faith of the first monotheist, Abraham. When the Angel Gabriel revealed God's message to Muhammad, it was a call for total submission to the one and only God and for the implementation of His will as revealed in its complete form one final time.

Muhammad, born in Mecca around 570, was left an orphan at the age of six. He was also poor, and who could have guessed the course his life would take? Muslims

The Islamic Foundation of Toronto.

believe that Muhammad serves not only as God's human instrument in revealing God's word but also as the model or ideal all believers should emulate.

As the genesis of God's revelation to Muhammad, the Qur'an gives the basic commandments which are similar to the Ten Commandments of the Bible. The daily prayer of the Muslims is based on the first surah (chapter) of the Qur'an. It is similar to the Lord's Prayer. Muslims ask in this prayer for help in following the straight path. Muslim ritual obligations include:

• *Shahadah*: The profession of faith by which every Muslim must proclaim that "There is no God but GOD (Allah) and Muhammad is the messenger of God."

• *Salat*: Five times a day Muslims are called to prayer by the muezzin atop a mosque's minaret. Facing in the direction of Mecca, at daybreak, noon, mid-afternoon, sunset, and evening, they recall the revelation of the Qur'an. Depending on the time of day, each prayer consists of two to four prostrations. Each one begins with "God is most great."

• *Zakat*: A payment of an alms tax or poor tithe, this is both an individual and communal requirement. It is assessed as a share of accumulated wealth and assets, not just income.

• *Sawm*: During Ramadan, the ninth month of the Islamic calendar, all healthy adult Muslims must abstain from food, drink, and sexual activity from sunrise to sunset. This is a time for expressing gratitude for God's guidance and for the atonement of past sins — a time of reflection and spiritual discipline.

• *Hajj*: Every adult Muslim who is physically and financially able must make a pilgrimage, at least once in his or her lifetime, to Mecca, birthplace of Muhammad. The focus of the pilgrimage is the cube-shaped Kaaba, the house of God which contains the black stone that was given to Abraham by the angel Gabriel. It is a symbol of God's covenant with Ishmael, son of Abraham and Hagar and, by association, with the Muslim community. As with prayer, the pilgrimage requires ritual purification, symbolized by the wearing of white garments. The pilgrimage ends in the celebration of the Feast of Sacrifice, which commemorates God's command to Abraham to sacrifice his son Ishmael. At the end of the pilgrimage, many of the faithful will visit Muhammad's tomb in the mosque at Medina.

Like many earlier pioneers, in the last several decades of the twentieth century Muslims from all corners of the globe have arrived in Ontario and other parts of Canada in search of a better economic life. Like earlier pioneers as well, they have confronted new and different challenges. After the long preceding age of the Canadian fur trade had already transformed the world of the province's first peoples, it was an often harsh and difficult physical environment that most challenged the early settlers of Upper Canada. More recent Islamic new arrivals have had to face the gauntlet of a more established and unfamiliar cultural environment, which can bring on a deep sense of isolation. As in other such cases, fundamental beliefs have been challenged by an increasingly open and permissive mainstream society, with its roots in a still youthful but also quite different kind of past, with different cultural traditions.

Thanks in part to the struggles of earlier pioneers, the same open society also believes in religious freedom and the mixed community. Like their predecessors, the Islamic pioneers of today at first lacked places of worship, but quickly rallied in small groups to practice their faith in warehouses and the basements of homes. Soon mosques were springing up in Toronto and other larger Ontario cities. Most of the old pioneers in the nineteenth century knew that their ties with the old country were broken: they would never return to their roots and quickly lost touch. In the early twenty-first century, a host of advances in transportation and communications technology have meant that new arrivals of all faiths can maintain closer connections with families, friends, and institutions in their countries of origin.

With at least this kind of support behind it, the present large, pristine, white cement-stone building of The Islamic Foundation of Toronto, near the intersection of Nugget

Avenue and Markham Road, began to take shape in 1989. An imposing edifice, it is not only a place of worship but also a centre for a wide range of Islamic cultural activities. One wing of the building houses a progressive elementary school. Well-trained teachers wearing the traditional *hijab* or head covering are in charge of some 270 pupils who follow the latest Ontario curriculum as well as Islamic and Arabic studies. This very modern institution has a cavernous gymnasium and a large common room where the congregation can hold social events. Arched windows allow light to stream into the well-stocked library.

A mortuary is located in the basement of the building. Burials usually take place the same day as or the morning after death. Regardless of wealth or status all are given the same treatment. A *kafan* (two pieces of white cloth) shroud the body. After funerary prayers are said, the plain coffin is borne to a special section in Pine Ridge Memorial Gardens, to the east in the Town of Ajax, in Durham Region. Care is taken to see that the head is facing in the direction of Mecca.

The heart of the Islamic Foundation building is beneath the open focal dome: the *sahn*. This large, clear central area can accommodate the hundreds who come to prayer. The *mihrab*, a recess in the eastern wall, indicates to the worshippers that they are facing Mecca. From his place in the *minbar*, also in the eastern end of the sanctuary, an imam will give the Friday sermon. The slender minaret is reached by an entrance inside the building. Although an elevator services the main areas, the imams must ascend the winding staircase five times a day.

The establishment of a fair and just society on earth was one motivation of Muhammad's mission. Just as the twentieth century came to an end, the Toronto Islamic community's public-spirited response to the tragic death of the five-year-old girl, Farah Khan, showed something of what deeply held religious beliefs can still mean, even in an age of jet airplanes and computer technology. In February 2000, more than one thousand people of many different faiths attended a funeral for the young girl in a Toronto mosque, bearing witness to the continuing solidarity of the life of the spirit, no matter what form it takes, in Ontario's capital city today.

53. Hoa Nghiem Temple (Buddhist), 1992
1278 Gerrard Street East, at Greenwood

Be lamps unto yourselves and seek no external refuge.
Hold fast to the Truth as a lamp and a refuge.
Gautama Buddha (circa 563–483 B.C.)

$\mathcal{S}$outhwest of the Islamic Foundation building on Nugget Avenue, in the east end of the old Toronto inner city, the practices of another great world religion from the east mingle with memories of an unsettling war — at the Hoa Nghiem Buddhist Temple on Gerrard Street, at Greenwood Avenue.

Although not the only Buddha, his followers consider Gautama Buddha to be the finder rather than the founder of their religion. They look upon him as not only the profoundest of religious philosophers but the greatest of human beings as well.

The term Buddha means "the Awakened or Enlightened One" — qualities that must be rediscovered by each Buddha. Impermanence of all things is one of the cardinal tenets of Buddhism. Another outstanding precept is that truth is its own proof and must be verifiable. There is no external deity in heaven or on earth to whom one is answerable. Salvation is not a blessing conferred by a Higher Being; it is the outcome of self-examination and meditation. One is responsible solely to oneself and the onus is on the individual to reach a state of nirvana.

The son of an ancient king or chieftain, Siddharta Gautama enjoyed all the privileges of royalty as a youth. He was born a northern Indian prince at Lumbini Garden in present-day Nepal, and his birthplace is still an important centre of Buddhist pilgrimage. It is said that his mother conceived him after dreaming that the future Buddha descended from heaven in the form of a white elephant and entered her womb. She died a week after giving birth. The child was reared by his mother's sister, who was also one of his father's wives. Many years later, renouncing his own wife and infant son, Gautama began a period of self-denial. For the next forty-five years, he preached a way of life that would bring enlightenment and compassion to all.

Though it has very little architectural distinction, Hoa Nghiem Temple on Gerrard Street is home to one of the largest Vietnamese Buddhist congregations in Canada today. It is a low, flat-topped oblong structure that no longer resembles the former home of an

Hoa Nghiem Temple, Toronto.

east Toronto club which once entertained quite different patrons. But it does not remotely resemble a traditional Buddhist temple either. Only the name emblazoned on the dark overhang of the white walls makes clear what the building is now. Inside, kneeling in front of individual prayer stands, men and women join together in worship every Sunday. Younger people in the contemporary dress of their new country blend with elders wearing the traditional robes of the homeland. They all face toward the statues of three Buddhas, who represent the past, the present, and the future.

The congregation of the Hoa Nghiem Temple is made up of Vietnamese refugees of Chinese descent. These new Buddhist pioneers in Ontario today have come from a land torn by strife. A former part of the old French global empire, Vietnam went on to endure untold suffering in a civil war that eventually came to involve the United States — and would have side-effects in Canada as well. With the end of the Vietnam War in the mid-1970s, and the reunification of north and south, the two million people of Chinese descent in Vietnam felt especially threatened. A mass exodus began. It has been estimated that some fifty thousand refugees eventually found their way to Canada.

The Reverend Pho Timh, the first woman of her religion to be ordained in Canada, was one of these refugees. Fearing for her life, the young Pho Timh fled her native land in a small boat, with forty men and eight women. While wallowing at sea, they were beset by pirates. The men were badly beaten, and the terrified women huddled together under a tarpaulin. After six days, the boat came to rest on a small island off the coast of Malaysia. To the refugees' horror, there was no fresh water on the island. Banana palms, sometimes cooked in salt water, were their only food. After twenty-eight days Pho Timh and her companions, unable to stand, were finally picked up by a United Nations rescue mission. Perhaps Quan The Am, the Buddhist symbol of female compassion, was watching over them. Several refugees believe they saw her appear over the storm-tossed sea when their tiny craft was in danger of floundering.

Taken to Kuala Lumpur in Malaysia, Pho Timh tried for a year to get accepted as a refugee by various national states. For a long time she did not apply to Canada because she had been told that it was a land of ice and snow. At last, in desperation, she was willing to take a chance. Upon applying, she was told that some ability to speak French was a requirement for immigrating to her chosen destination of Montréal. Having grown up in a country with at least a certain experience of the language, she quickly learned enough French phrases to be accepted.

In spite of homesickness and disorientation, Pho Timh has found her own bridge across the great gap that still lies between the cultures of her old and new countries. Already a university graduate, she enrolled at McGill University in Montréal, where she earned one master's degree in religion and another in education. Today she works in the Canadian national office of the Chanh Giac Vietnamese Association. She is grateful for the freedom she enjoys in her new country.

On a Sunday morning in the spring of the year 2000, Pho Timh from Montréal made a special appearance at Hoa Nghiem Temple on Gerrard Street in Toronto. Offerings of vegetarian food and flowers were laid on the altar, where puffs of scented smoke drifted up from burning sticks of incense. Saffron-robed priests led the congregation in prayer. Separated from the main sanctuary, a special offering of food was laid out on an altar under the pictures of family members who have died. Dressed in the white of mourning, grieving relatives paid tribute to their loved ones.

Buddhism has brought comfort and wisdom to people in different parts of the world for well over two thousand years. One senses that the younger people at Hoa Nghiem Temple are already moving closer to the wider society. As in earlier eras, the new pioneers' children who grow up in Canada quickly become much like the other children among whom they grow up. But the other children also become a little more like them. The wider world of the mixed community itself is always changing. That is another interesting thing about the present-day life of the spirit in Ontario, as it looks out somewhat quizzically at just what the twenty-first century might finally bring.

Epilogue

$\mathcal{I}$t may seem odd to end this collection of Ontario pioneer places of worship with yet another place in the province's capital city. But Toronto still has one or two fewer representatives than its current population and economic role might suggest. I have already paid a great deal of attention to older, smaller churches scattered throughout southern Ontario's smaller towns and villages. Partly because of its greater population importance in the nineteenth century, eastern Ontario is especially well represented. We have been as far north as Thunder Bay and Moosonee, and I have stressed the continuing attractions of such places as Petrolia in the deep southwest.

There is similarly a rather long-established Toronto place of worship that brings this journey through Ontario history, via its religious institutions, to as much of a conclusion as it can have, or perhaps even needs. The unsurprising point of this particular story is that all places of worship function as social gathering places as well. "Pioneering spirit" is about building human communities that last over time. As it is written in Proverbs 29:18: "Where there is no vision, the people perish."

54. WoodGreen United Church, 1959
875 Queen Street East, west of Carlaw, Toronto

To every thing there is a season, and a time
to every purpose under the heaven.
Ecclesiastes 3:1

$\mathcal{T}$he story of WoodGreen United Church began in the countryside east of the Don River, in a much smaller City of Toronto than the one we know today, not long after

Old WoodGreen Church, which used to stand
at the corner of Queen and Strange.

the Canadian confederation of 1867. The story is still going on but, as in other parts of Ontario, both the area in which it began and the church itself have been through many changes.

In the beginning, in any case, a place of worship known as the Don Bridge Church, steeped in the traditions of Old Ontario Methodism, organized Sunday school classes in a building on Queen Street east of the Don in the later nineteenth century. Apparently, the first superintendent was a Presbyterian who liked to recruit other Presbyterians. There seems a whimsical sense in which, for a time, the church was a forerunner of the eventual union between Methodists and Presbyterians in the United Church of Canada.

A subsequent disagreement between the two groups led a faction of so-called Wesleyan Methodists to strike out more clearly on their own. Their first pastor, the Reverend John Carroll, was dismayed to find an initial membership of only seven persons. But this hard-working and dedicated man quickly increased the size of the congregation. He recorded that, during his first year, he preached 137 sermons, made 1372 calls, attended 123 prayer meetings, met classes 51 times, dispensed the Lord's Supper seven times, held four love feasts, baptized 34 children, married one couple, and buried another.

Reverend Carroll strove not only to stimulate the religious life of his congregation but also to bring people to God by his own counsels and admonitions. In the midst of all his other duties, he still had the energy to lead his growing congregation in constructing a new church building at the corner of Queen and Strange Streets. In October 1875, the opening services of the new church were conducted by two eminent leaders of Wesleyan Methodism, Dr. Enoch Wood and Dr. Anson Green. (The name "WoodGreen" derives from their surnames.)

Over the next fifteen years, the congregation grew rapidly, along with its surrounding neighbourhood. The "Riverdale" area east of the Don River was starting to attract new factories in the city's rising industrial economy — along with many of the people who worked in these factories. Enlarged and renovated premises for WoodGreen Church at Queen and Strange streets were opened in January 1890.

In the midst of its continuing growth, the WoodGreen Methodists and some neighbouring Presbyterians lived through a devastating tragedy at a weekend outing in Niagara Falls. Travelling at breakneck speed, a trolley car in which the group was riding lost control and plunged off the track. The choirmaster and the treasurer of WoodGreen were among the thirteen killed. Another eighty people were injured.

Perhaps partly because of past disagreements between local Methodists and Presbyterians, WoodGreen Methodist Church did not join the new United Church of Canada until the early 1930s. By this point the Great Depression was well underway, and it had hit the factories and their employees in the area east of the Don River especially hard. At the height of the Depression, it is said, some sixty percent of the population in the neighbourood was on city relief. The strictly spiritual concerns of WoodGreen United Church began to be overshadowed by the more immediate needs of the community, right outside the church's front door.

With thoughts of this sort on their minds, two WoodGreen members, Mr. and Mrs. Frank Costella, deeded their house on Boulton Avenue to the church, on the understanding that it would be used for both the church and the neighbourhood. In addition to providing housing for another hard-working and dedicated minister, Reverend Ray McCleary, the bottom floor was often filled with "shivering derelicts" who had drifted in off the street. (Reverend McCleary would say, "When I moved in, I threw away the key.") To offset the neighbourhood's grim 1930s surroundings, Reverend McCleary also persuaded his congregation to paint the doors of both the church and the house on Boulton Avenue a brilliant red. Despite some early unneighbourly comment, this proved an inspiration for a tradition of community service that Reverend McCleary launched with the establishment of WoodGreen Community Centre in 1937.

WoodGreen Community Centre began in Reverend McCleary's house on Boulton Avenue, with the brilliant red door. It would continue to operate from the house until 1947, when it at last acquired a more suitable building of its own. By the late 1940s some degree of prosperity had returned to the Toronto industrial neighbourhood east of the Don River, but the area would never exactly recover from the Great Depression. By the middle of the twentieth century it had begun a new long history as a so-called inner-city neighbourhood in transition. There continued to be a great need for the services the WoodGreen Community Centre was providing.

Even with its 1890 renovations, the old 1875 building of WoodGreen United Church at Queen and Strange streets was now in need of substantial repair. Rather than restore the old structure, the congregation decided to find a new site for an up-to-date new church and an accompanying "Neighbourhood House." Land on the south side of Queen Street between Logan and Booth avenues was purchased, immediately east of the present WoodGreen Community Centre building. A committee was set up to raise the required funds. It was decided that public funds would not be solicited; a private campaign would suffice.

In fact, WoodGreen United has benefited from the generosity of many private contributors over the years. Prominent people have donated both time and money to the work of the Church and the Community Centre, and so have people whose proudest distinction is that they live in the neighbourhood. It can be said that the tradition goes as far back as Reverend John Carroll in the later nineteenth century. One day he was driving home over the Don Bridge in his horse-drawn buggy when he overtook a young man dressed in working clothes. The young man beckoned for Reverend Carroll to stop. Without giving his name, he shyly tendered a $5 bill (a quite enormous sum in those days). "This is for your church," the young man said, and quietly slipped away.

According to legend, during the planning of the new church building and Neighbourhood House in the 1950s, a senior minister kept impulsively bursting in with some new concept for the project. When he went on his annual leave, the committee rendered a prayer of thanks that they could finally complete the work in peace. In 1959, the congregation of WoodGreen United Church formed a colourful parade as it marched along Queen Street from the old premises at Strange Street to the modern building near the corner of Logan Avenue. It was a day of great rejoicing and renewal.

As the 1960s gathered momentum, the inner-city neighbourhood in transition would undergo still further transitions. By the early 1970s new arrivals of Chinese ancestry had begun to settle in the wider area, in increasing numbers. By this point as well the factories of an earlier age had begun to move out. The old city was "de-industrializing," as new, more up-to-date manufacturing plants sprang up on the peripheries of the sprawling Greater Toronto Area. In the 1980s and 1990s the Riverdale area east of the Don River became increasingly attractive to younger urban dwellers, looking for affordable housing close to the megapolitan downtown.

Today there are three WoodGreen Red Door Shelters operating in the Toronto inner city — all descendants, so to speak, of Reverend McCleary's little house on Boulton Avenue in the 1930s. One of them is linked to the present WoodGreen United Church building on Queen Street by a delightful garden. Still lovingly tended by members of the church, it provides a tranquil area for passersby to pause and reflect. Benches in front of the Community Centre next door provide a resting place for tired feet. It is the Community Centre that manages the Red Door Shelters. At the three sites, 240 beds are provided for homeless families, refugees, the elderly, abused women and their

Present-day WoodGreen United Church on the right. The WoodGreen Neighbourhood House is on the left. The two buildings are attached.

children, and young mothers with newborn babies — all linked with other family services provided by the Toronto Police, the Children's Aid Society, Public Health, and the United Way.

The Community Centre has in fact evolved into a large and complex social service organization, and is now heavily funded by governments (though recent reductions from this source have also been prompting a return to earlier traditions of private fund-raising). It has staff who speak English, Cantonese, Mandarin, Chao-chou, and Vietnamese. It runs a childcare service, an after-school program, and a summer day camp. Its Employment and Training Services offer job-search help, particularly for young people and recent immigrants. The Mandarin Outreach Program helps to ease the transition to Canadian society for new arrivals of Chinese ancestry who speak Mandarin. The Community Centre also manages several affordable housing buildings and several programs for neighbourhood seniors. There is much more that could be told as well.

WoodGreen United Church in its own right runs an annual income tax clinic. It hosts a community meal that feeds between 130 and 150 homeless people every third Tuesday. A craft group meets every Thursday. A drop-in centre is open each Tuesday for lunch and cards. The church holds community Bible study groups, and keeps its sanctuary open every Wednesday, from noon to one o'clock, for individual meditation and prayer.

Like other places of worship across the province started by older and newer pioneers alike —First Nations, Christians, Jews, Buddhists, Hindus, Muslims, Sikhs, and on and on —WoodGreen United has pressed ahead through all the changes in the world around it by keeping faith with the community in which it lives. Although the spiritual needs of the congregation are of prime importance, the church is still paying heed to the old motto of the Red Door: "The Red Door helps those who need help to help themselves." The congregation at WoodGreen United has acted on the words of Jesus Christ as recounted in Matthew 25: 35–36: "I was hungry and you fed me, thirsty and you gave me a drink; I was a stranger and you received me in your homes, naked and you clothed me; I was sick and you took care of me, in prison and you visited me."

This seems to me to summarize something that has been true of all those who have been pioneering all the various lives of the spirit that go to make up the mixed community in Ontario today. The life of the spirit is not just about the life of the spirit. It is also about making the world a better place.

Locations

NOTE: All places of worship are indicated by the number assigned to them in the headings in the text.

NORTHERN ONTARIO

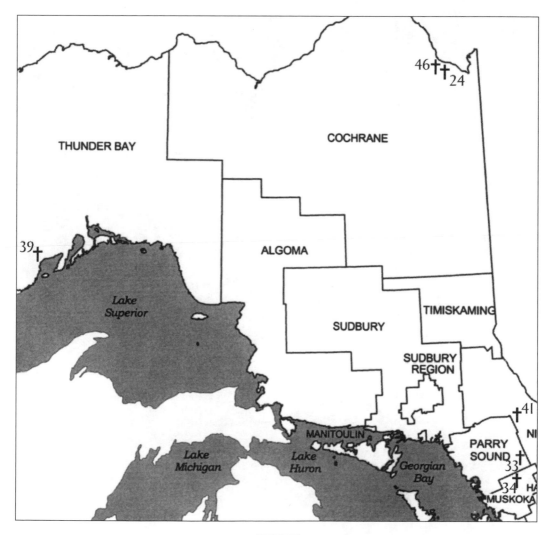

SOUTHERN ONTARIO — WEST

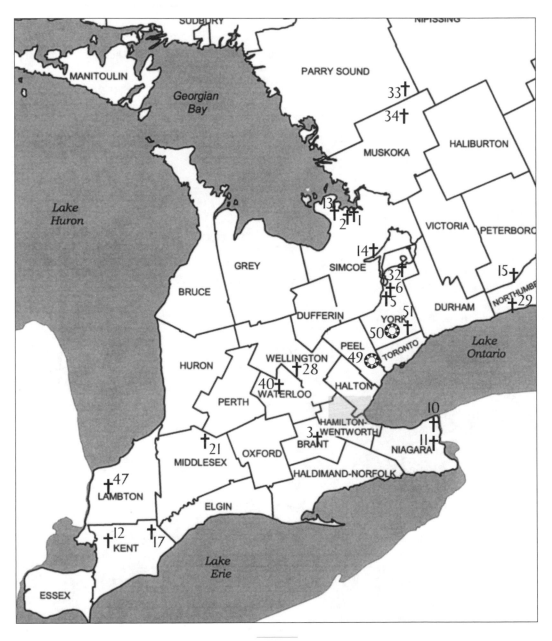

SOUTHERN ONTARIO — EAST

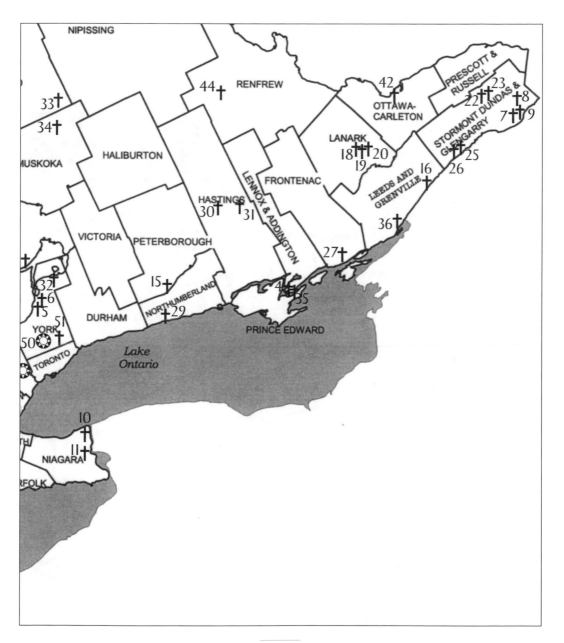

GREATER TORONTO AREA

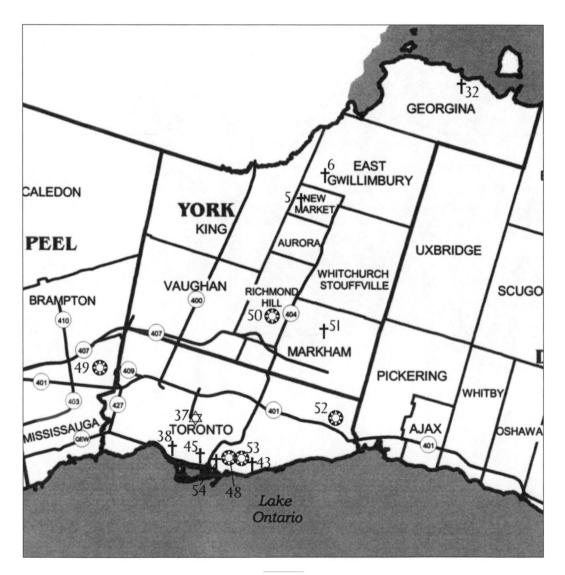

Further Reading

BOOKS AND ARTICLES

Batty, Beatrice. *Forty-two Years Amongst the Indians and Eskimo: Pictures from the Life of the Right Reverend John Horden, First Bishop of Moosonee.* 2nd ed. London: Religious Tract Society, [1894?].

Berton, Pierre. *The Dionne Years: A Thirties Melodrama.* Toronto: McClelland and Stewart, 1977.

Burkholder, L.J. *A Brief History of the Mennonites in Ontario: Giving a Description of Conditions in Early Ontario, the Coming of the Mennonites Into Canada, Settlements, Congregations, Conferences, Other Activities, and Nearly 400 Ordinations.* Toronto: Livingstone Press, 1935.

Byers, Mary, Jan Kennedy, Margaret McBurney, and the Junior League of Toronto. *Rural Roots: Pre-Confederation Buildings of the York Region of Ontario.* Toronto: University of Toronto Press, 1976.

Collins, Gilbert. *Guide Book to the Historic Sites of the War of 1812.* Toronto: Dundurn Press, 1998.

Conze, Edward. *Buddhist Scriptures.* Harmondsworth, Middlesex: Penguin Books, 1960.

Cooper, John Irwin. *Ontario's First Century: 1610–1713.* Montréal: The Lawrence Lande Foundation, McGill University, 1978.

Craig, Gerald M. *Upper Canada: The Formative Years 1784–1841.* Toronto: McClelland and Stewart, 1963.

Epp, Frank H. *1786–1920: The History of a Separate People.* Vol. 1 of *Mennonites in Canada.* Toronto: Macmillan of Canada, 1974.

Esposito, John L. *Islam: The Straight Path.* New York: Oxford University Press, 1998.

Farah, Caesar E. *Islam: Beliefs and Observances.* 6th ed. Hauppauge, New York: Barron's, 2000.

Gray, Elma E. *Wilderness Christians: The Moravian Mission to the Delaware Indians.* Toronto: Macmillan, 1956.

Hart, Arthur Daniel. *The Jew in Canada: A Complete Record of Canadian Jewry from the Days of the French Régime to the Present Time.* Toronto: Jewish Publications, 1926.

Hett, Francis Paget. *Georgina: A Type Study of Early Settlement and Church Building in Upper Canada.* Toronto: Macmillan, 1939.

Holmes, Jean. *Times to Remember in Elzevir Township.* Ontario: The Council, 1984.

Ivison, Stuart and Fred Rosser. *The Baptists in Upper and Lower Canada Before 1820.* Toronto: University of Toronto Press, 1956.

Kelley, Thomas P. *The Black Donnellys.* Willowdale, Ontario: Firefly Books, 1993.

Kertzer, Morris Norman. *What Is a Jew?* Rev. ed. New York: Macmillan, 1972.

Knipe, David M. *Hinduism: Experiments in the Sacred.* San Francisco: HarperSanFrancisco, 1991.

Landon, Fred. "When Uncle Tom's Cabin Came to Canada." *Ontario History,* xliv (1) January 1952, pp. 1-5.

MacRae, Marion. *Hallowed Walls: Church Architecture in Upper Canada.* Toronto: Clarke, Irwin, 1975.

Millar, Nancy. *Once Upon a Tomb: Stories from Canadian Graveyards.* Calgary: Fifth House, 1997.

Ondaatje, Kim. *Small Churches of Canada.* Toronto: Lester & Orphen Dennys, 1982.

Preyde, Susan and James Preyde. *Steeple Chase: Ontario's Historic Churches.* Erin, Ontario: Boston Mills Press, 1991.

Pryke, Susan. *Explore Muskoka.* Erin, Ontario: Boston Mills Press, 1987. Reprinted 1999.

Rosten, Leo Calvin, comp. *Religions of America: Ferment and Faith in an Age and Crisis: A New Guide and Almanac.* New York: Simon and Schuster, 1975.

Russell, Foster Meharry. *What a Friend We Have in Jesus.* Belleville, Ontario: Mika Publishing Company, 1981.

Winks, Robin W. *The Blacks in Canada: A History.* Montréal: McGill–Queen's University Press, 1971.

Woodcock, George. *The Century That Made Us: Canada 1814–1914.* Toronto: Oxford University Press, 1989.

Woodham-Smith, Cecil. *Florence Nightingale, 1820–1910.* New York: McGraw-Hill, 1951.

Zurakowska, Anna, ed. *The Proud Inheritance: Ontario's Kaszuby.* Ottawa: Polish Heritage Institute-Kaszuby, 1991.

PAMPHLETS AND OTHER LOCALLY PUBLISHED MATERIAL

Bickle, Ethel F. *In and Around Canton.* Published by Ethel F. Bickle, n.d.

Blackburn, Alma, Blanche Sandford, and Alma Moorcroft. *Pilgrimage of Faith: 150 Years of History of the Churches in Madoc Township and Village, 1824–1974.* Madoc, Ontario: Madoc Review Ltd., 1975.

Cosens, Donald L., ed. *The Donnelly Tragedy, 1880–1980.* London, Ontario: Phelps Publishing Company, 1980.

Dedication Souvenir: To Commemorate the Opening of the New Holy Blossom Temple, 1938. n.p.

Farr, D.M.L. *A Church in the Glebe: St. Matthew's, Ottawa, 1898–1988: A History Prepared for the Occasion of the 90th Anniversary of St. Matthew's Church.* Ottawa: St. Matthew's Anglican Church, 1988.

Historical Notations, 1834 Onward. Sibbald Point, Ontario: St. George's Church, n.d.

A History, St. Thomas Church, Shanty Bay. n.p., n.d.

Hope Township Pastoral Charge of the United Church of Canada. *United in Hope: A History of the Present Congregations and Their Antecedents.* Hope Township, Ontario: Hope Township Pastoral Charge; Haynes Printing, [1975?].

Lamb, J. William. *William Losee: Ontario's Pioneer Methodist Missionary.* Adolphustown, Ontario: Board of Trustees of the Old Hay Bay Church, 1974.

McArthur, Emily. *Children of Peace: The History of a Novel Sect in York County.* York Pioneer and Historical Society pamphlet, [1898?].

Reynolds, Arthur G. *The Story of the Hay Bay Church 1792–1964*. Picton, Ontario: Picton Gazette Publishing Company, 1964.

St. James-on-the-Lines, 1836, Garrison Church of Penetanguishene. n.p., n.d.

Shortt, Edward, ed. *Perth Remembered*. Perth, Ontario: Printed by Mortimer for the Perth Museum, 1967.

Sneyd, Robert F. *Broken Glass: Shards of Battle Become a Living Memorial*. Printed by Hume Reproduction Centres, Toronto, 1994.

Warschauer, Heinz. *The Story of Holy Blossom Temple*. Toronto: The Author, 1956.

SELECTED WEBSITES

Anglican Church of Canada (Ontario)	http://www.ontario.anglican.ca
Catholic Canada Directory	http://catholicanada.com
Chapel of the Mohawks	http://www.geocities.com/chriskarkare/chapel.html
Circuit Rider (Hay Bay)	http://www3.sympatico.ca/dgenge/HistBQ.html
Historic Plaques of Ontario	http://www.waynecook.com/historiclist.html
Martyrs' Shrine, Midland	http://www.jesuits.ca/martyrs-shrine
Official Donnelly Home Page	http://www.donnellys.com
Presbyterian Church in Canada	http://www.presbyterian.ca
St. Anne's Anglican Church, Toronto	http://www.stannes.on.ca
St. James the Apostle Church, Perth	http://www.superaje.com/~stjames
Sainte-Marie Among the Hurons	http://www.saintemarieamongthehurons.on.ca
St. Mary's Church, Wilno	http://www.wilno.com
St. Matthew's Church, Ottawa	http://www.stmatthewsottawa.on.ca
St. Raphaels Ruins	http://www.glen-net.ca/raphaels
St. Thomas Church, Moose Factory	http://www.nt.net/moosonee/moose.htm
St. Thomas Church, Shanty Bay	http://www.bconnex.net/~elebrown
Sharon Temple	http://home.interhop.net/~aschrauwe/sharon.html
Sikh Traditions in Ontario	http://collections.ic.gc.ca/magic/mt36.html
St. Andrew's Church, Williamstown	http://www.glen-net.ca/st-andrews-ucc
United Church of Canada	http://www.uccan.org
WoodGreen Community Centre of Toronto	http://www.woodgreen.org

Index